Older Brother the Other

By Peter Koren

Published by GLOWING LIGHT LTD
2025 Edition
PaperBack
ISBN: 978-1-0670653-4-8

Older Brother the Other 1
THE OTHER BROTHER 5
   The Children of God 31
   Peter Walked on the Water 45
   The God Particle 51
THE TEMPLE 57
   The Collective Consciousness of Mankind 63
   One New Man!!! 71
   Little Children 83
   The Obedience of Christ 95
   Diversity meets the Other 115
   Light Love and Peace 141
A LONG WAY OFF 149

Copyright © 2025

All rights reserved worldwide. No part of this publication may be replicated, redistributed, or given away in any form without the prior written consent of the author/publisher or the terms relayed to you herein.

While every precaution has been taken in the preparation of this book, the publisher assumes no responsibility for errors or omissions,

or for damages resulting from the use of the information contained herein.

INTRODUCTION

Well how do two very opposite brothers get along?

They don't!

However, with God all things are possible.

God works in these two a way of mystery.
One who is very religious, on his high horse and the other; well he is reckless, wayward, you have heard about him; the prodigal.

What can we say about them?
How does God bring peace between these two?

Read on.

"Older Brother the Other"

A sequel to the Prodigal Son

The Other.

Could well be the Prodigal.
Being the other from the older brothers perspective.
He considers the Prodigals actions as putting him outside the sanctity of the fathers home and underserving to be accepted.
Meanwhile the older brother kept to the laws of the household and didn't go astray faithfully serving the father.

THE OTHER BROTHER

We have heard about the prodigal son but who is the other brother?

Copyright © March 2019

Is he your friendly smiling banker who approves your credit line, or he could be a policeman ticketing the speeding driver just over that limit.

Maybe a priest who lends a listening ear to your confession, or maybe he is in close proximity as a neighbor; or he could be a parking ticket warden, or just the guy you see in church who smiles on Sunday.

The Other Brother is a skilled operator and securely balances within the ethical upright, for all intentional purposes he appears to be a model citizen and he wouldn't dream of rocking the boat.

Certainly, he could be the one who generally keeps out of public mischief, he aims to please the authorities; earning his place and a good name in society.
He may not peak as someone among them, but he is somewhere in the ranks and has learnt the right moves, inwardly he believes that he should be elevated a little more up the corporate ladder, well above the undeserving, non-achiever.
The other brother could be the guy who strives for recognition, he admires those above him who have achieved corporate stardom, wishing to achieve the status of conducting seminars to the masses on the formulas of success.

He deftly climbs up the moral pyramid and doesn't go off the rails on decadent binges; he avoids the wild party animals that just want to forget their troubles and get wasted.

He has learnt the secret codes by attending well-crafted paths to success seminars and he is convinced that now he is on track for a much earned promotion, working hard with the keys of advancement in the ranks of the respectful.

He may be the one who serves consistently at church, maybe not out as a front man with a microphone, this is something he is not sure about, wondering just when he will be recognised and make his well earnt break, well, at least he knows that he does have a good and steady record.
He can be a she, so it works in both genders just shift the roles to fit.
In fact he could be you, or he could be me!!!

If he was graded, he would be awarded an easy C+ and maybe achieve A- tops on a good day, if the assessors were in a particularly generous mood.
That's OK, he has done the basics and he knows he is good enough and not on the ship of fools on the road to nowhere.

He has a security, knowing that he has a good, clean record and in that he is satisfied, as he knows that there are others that have missed the mark and they have fallen off the edge and won't stay with the program.

So, why should they be accepted with open arms?
They slink back in after a shameful episode of reckless living! They have lost the plot and should be back in boot camp until they prove themselves to be worthy!
They are the prodigals and are wayward, undeserving and have been reckless and ended up in the pits!

If the repentant backslider manages to accelerate up the ranks in the church system, which includes an outrageous testimony with Hollywood style stunts, this is very troubling indeed.

Accepting an undisciplined, wayward believer who has completely blown it and has finally come to his senses into <u>any</u> position, above my level, just isn't right!
Internal self talk of the other brother could also go like this:
"Sure, we celebrate that he has come to his senses, long overdue and great he got out of the pig pen, well you couldn't go any lower, so start where you belong!!!

I have been a good member of the church, not living in shameful ways, so where is my robe? Where is my party?"
I have copped the flack for being a good person and then rejected for not being part of the social addicts, party mad world. I don't fit into that scene anyway, never have, they are on the wrong track and I just can't go there."
"Brother! You didn't earn it!"
<u>Possible thoughts from the other brother when confronted by the reckless prodigal who returns to the ranks with much celebration. (most likely the prodigal becomes a zealous evangelist, eager to see others like him set free)</u>

The other brother was in close vicinity to the Father, but in some ways he was disconnected as well.
How could this be when he spent a lifetime in the right place and did not stray into a life of corruption and reckless living?

His record is commendable and he would be in a better position than the wayward son, as he remains close to the standards expected by the Father and doesn't get into trouble which leads to moral failure.

To be accepted as a son or daughter of God is the best place anyone can be, this is true security and in that place of acceptance we can truly live and serve with great joy and true energy from a well of living water which is powered by the love of God.

1 John 3:1
[1] See what great love the Father has lavished on us, that we should be called children of God! And that is what we are! The reason the world does not know us is that it did not know Him.

The truth is *"both of the brothers are a little bit you and a little bit me"*, we all tend to go astray, leaning towards the prodigal like sheep wandering, or flip the other way; working self-righteously to be good enough in our own estimation of how things should be.

Remember the Apostle Paul said do not judge the weaker brother, or also don't judge the one who practices certain religious traditions.

We are to accept where each other are at and appreciate, that we are all at different stages of our journey to mature as sons and daughters of God; we need to help each other and encourage one another to reach the mark and our individual destiny.

We all have a background and makeup of different cultural diversities and personality types and all of us have our limitations, of not knowing fully who we really are in Christ, therefore we can all benefit from one another, as we all have our gift and place to help the whole body function together as one.

The desire of the Father is that we all come into a closer relationship with Him and have a real freedom to enjoy His blessings and favour to be the best person that we can be, partaking in His wonderful grace in great joy and peace and receiving the Fathers immeasurable, boundless love.
Yes the prodigal wasted his inheritance and destroyed his life, with living for pleasure and looking for the high life and recognition from the world and the party scene. He was insecure and felt the need to find his identity in the market place and make a name for himself.
If he remained there in the pits, then his end would have been destruction and a great loss,

far away from the protection and blessing of the Father in Heaven.

He needed to come to his senses and what change his mind – which is the definition of - *to repent* = change your ways and return to the right pathway.

Really, how could he do that, he has demonstrated that he is incapable of making right choices and has lived a shameful existence outside of the ways of God?

Only the Father can accept him back, based on a given birth right or the family name and not on any merit of his own actions. The Father extends the invitation to be restored back into the family with the benefits of being a son, which has always been offered to the prodigal. There remains the barrier to receiving Gods undeserved favour to all, choice; we all have a God given free will which God does not violate. The prodigal and everyone else needs to make a free will choice to accept their place and remain within the family, receiving all of the benefits provided by the Fathers presence, continuing in His never ending love.

To be noted in the story of the prodigal, there is no mention of the Father immediately placing the wayward son in a position of responsibility; the focus is on being accepted back as a son, which will then position him to develop into the person of maturity in Christ.

So how can this wandering and unstable mind now live right and not stray off the track again into a life of destruction?

Galatians 2:20, 21
[20] I have been crucified with Christ; it is no longer I who live, but Christ lives in me; and the *life* which I now live in the flesh I live by faith in the Son of God, who loved me and gave Himself for me.
[21] I do not set aside the grace of God; for if righteousness *comes* through the law, then Christ died in vain."

The power to live right is in the place of being raised up with Christ by faith in the working of God in our lives, to transform us to be the person He predestined us to be in this world, having put off the body of a sinful lifestyle, our old ways of destructive living is buried with Christ and we are raised up in the new life.

The other brother, although he did not stray away from the place of the Fathers house, did not discover the freedom to celebrate that he is accepted as a son and can now freely partake of an inheritance that has already been provided.

He thought that if he follows the rules, he will receive his due inheritance as in a contract; his acceptance should then be from his dutiful efforts to win the blessings from the Father.

Does that mean that believers in Christ do not need to abide by the rules and disregard values, as there is no point, as we can't earn our place anyway?
Believers are sons and daughters of the Father by an inheritance given by the work of Jesus, who has legally gained our righteousness through the shedding of His blood to provide to us a new bloodline from the very DNA of Heaven, we can now by faith inherit righteousness and be the right person before Him. It is a relationship of love and respect, not based upon an independent performance of doing the right things. As we identify with Him in life, we still need to identify with His death, our old nature DNA patterns are put on the cross with Him in order that we make the trade for the new life in Him.
Not so bad, there still needs to be a trade off.

When we enter this world our natural bloodline and behaviour, performance came from the first Adam, who fell away from the righteousness and blessings of God. The first Adam became an independent creature, no longer subject to the right way of living that God is by nature, God is I AM and He is light and there is no shadow of turning in Him, He is the complete and perfect one by nature and the essence of pure love, He cannot fall, as He is complete within His own attributes.
When His creation Adam, made in His image became separated by taking the fruit of independent knowledge of good and evil,

Adam no longer was directed by the right ways of God, but became disconnected having his own independent nature, which is incapable of living a righteous life like God.
Best example, the first known to rebel from God, Satan or Lucifer and what is this fruit of independence like? Satan comes to kill, steal and destroy.

We all miss the mark somewhere without God, so He had to rescue us from ourselves and our inherited flawed bloodline, by sending Jesus to the cross to take the fallen nature on Himself, to legally accept and take from us the punishment or consequences of living separate to God and then He was risen again, into the resurrected righteousness of God, so that we can be partakers of the new life that God has provided for us, we are reconnected in nature to the Father in Heaven, who is pure and holy and now we can draw upon His goodness to be complete in Christ, Christ in us is our only hope of Glory.

Celebrating and being who we were created to be by our Father God is what pleases Him and we have access to these blessings by faith. We can be the person that we were originally designed to be and be transformed from the corruption of the fallen mankind DNA, which was contaminated by the disconnection from Gods way of life.

He won't reject His own creation, He loves who we are and wants us to celebrate with Him our true self and then just enjoy His company as we are fully accepted by the Father and we enter into and receive who we really are in Him by faith, not by trying to follow a set of rules alone, in independence from what has been provided to us by the cross. After the first Adam fell, the second Adam, who is Jesus our Saviour and King came to save us and set us free from the ways of an independent, corrupted spirit.

Our good works will now be in free flow from our spirit man, as this is who we really are and we live in the way and the truth and the life, which enables us to enter into Father God's, best plans of recovery for the fallen human race.

1 Peter 3:21
[21] There is also an antitype which now saves us—baptism (not the removal of the filth of the flesh, but the answer of a good conscience toward God), through the resurrection of Jesus Christ,

This is what saves us, when we enter into baptism with Jesus which doesn't just remove the acts of the fallen nature, but provides us with a clean slate and acceptance, by the power of the resurrection of Jesus working in us into a brand new man in Him.

1 Peter 3:22
²² who has gone into heaven and is at the right hand of God, angels and authorities and powers having been made subject to Him.

Resurrection life now flows in us from Jesus, who is at the Right Hand of the Father and He rules far above all of the powers that keeps us bound in the works of the fallen nature.

We now LIVE a new life above the powers of this world and not below them.

1 Peter 4:1, 2
¹ Therefore, since Christ suffered for us in the flesh, arm yourselves also with the same mind, for he who has suffered in the flesh has ceased from sin,
² that he no longer should live the rest of his time in the flesh for the lusts of men, but for the will of God.

Since we are now connected to the Father partaking in His DNA and the ability to live right, we have the Same Mind as Jesus, like when He was on the earth as a man being subject to His Heavenly Father.

Therefore, we no longer need to remain bound in the flesh and its lusts, through a baptism into the death of Jesus; we now have received His resurrection ability to enter into a righteous life style, provided by His resurrection from the dead. We identify with His death and since He carried our sins and weaknesses, we are now free to cease our life of sin and be living in the Will of God.

Our Reality is hope in our Victory!
Our Faith is Our Victory!
We abide in Victory!
1 John 4:17-21
17 Love has been perfected among us in this: that we may have boldness in the day of judgment; because as He is, so are we in this world.
18 There is no fear in love; but perfect love casts out fear, because fear involves torment. But he who fears has not been made perfect in love.
19 We love Him because He first loved us.
20 If someone says, "I love God," and hates his brother, he is a liar; for he who does not love his brother whom he has seen, how can he love God whom he has not seen?
21 And this commandment we have from Him: that he who loves God must love his brother also.

The Good News is although on the surface of things, we look a lot like the prodigal son in wayward behavior and escapism, or we look down on others from a proud heart like the other brother, the reality is that we need the love of the Father to motivate how we live.
We all know that we don't live like Jesus did remaining sinless, but when saved we are on a progression towards maturity and there is a conflict going on inside us to resist change and remain independent. However, as we have seen by the wayward son, this independence leads to destruction and food from the pig pen.

On the other hand, if we take on the attitude like the other brother who is very religious in his own eyes, which is another form of independence from God, we are judging others based on how we see others and from our own constructed set of situational ethics.

As He is love, so can we love, because He first loved us, despite our failures.

How then, can someone please tell me, does anyone born of God not become judgmental or rebellious?
Because it is Christ in us the hope of Glory that now lives in us and when we partake of these attributes of the love of God, we are no longer living in the attributes and characteristics of a self centred lifestyle.
Colossians 1:27
27 To them God willed to make known what are the riches of the glory of this mystery among the Gentiles: which is Christ in you, the hope of glory.

Indeed I believe it is a process, with some of the God kind of suddenlies, to turbo charge our transformation on the way, also in the right conditions and choices, we can help speed the process up and see fruit or as the case may be, allow it to be a long process, take the hard road, do you know what I mean?

Well a lot of tough human nature becomes stubborn and resistant, full of friction and the sparks of hard, resistant and metal grinding.

God please be patient with us?
Not always the easy path; as I can relate only too well, in the end sooner better than later, it is worth surrendering our independent ways and resist the urge to take the hard way.
The New Creation is a reality and the old has passed away.
As we are crucified with Him.
We now are resurrected with Him in life not death.

Remaining in this truth.
Abide in His grace and favour to be the person He created you to be.
We are now His workmanship created in Christ Jesus.
Ephesians 2:8-10
[8] For by grace you have been saved through faith, and that not of yourselves; it is the gift of God,
[9] not of works, lest anyone should boast.
[10] For we are His workmanship, created in Christ Jesus for good works, which God prepared beforehand that we should walk in them.
By grace we have been saved and this is not coming from our own works of an independent spirit, that sits on a high horse having its own set of rules and controls its own good and evil as one sees fit.

This is why the morals and standards of worldly, governing authorities, which are not based in the ways of God, shift and change to suit whatever agenda suits their preferences and plans.

We can now inherent in us the good works which we are predestined to walk in.

Very well then Mr Smarty, why aren't believers always living right by this awesome power available and demonstrating the life style of victory provided?
A question that may well be asked!!!
Why do the sons and daughters of God go through so many trials and setbacks as they develop their faith?
1 Peter 4:12
[12] ***Beloved, do not think it strange concerning the fiery trial which is to try you, as though some strange thing happened to you;***
We are thrown into a fiery trial and we better hope that there is someone with us who shines like the Son of God and the reality is that He is with us and in our hearts as believers, to bring us through the trials to victory.
1 Peter 1:6, 7
[6] ***In this you greatly rejoice, though now for a little while, if need be, you have been grieved by various trials,***
[7] ***that the genuineness of your faith, being much more precious than gold that perishes, though it is tested by fire, may be found to praise, honor, and glory at the revelation of Jesus Christ,***

Well a little while can seem like a life time!
While our faith is tested by fire – just what the doctor ordered you reckon!!!
I think I would prefer rest and recovery???

Our faith needs to be drawn out and sometimes it takes fire to refine what is a mixture of the pure seed with the old weeds coming to the surface during the trials. The impurities of the echo of our past life and internal struggles that leans towards independence from God, require refinement, as we habitually rely on our own judgements of right and wrong. If Jesus learned obedience while He was in human form and He was sinless, imagine what we require in comparison?
There is a lot of kicking and screaming going on, as children perform and we do need to learn to grow up and reach maturity; sometimes that means putting on a whole new mind set and perspective other than our own agendas, some of our ideas only profit our domain on this earth.

Our flesh nature might go berserk when heated up when all of the crazy stuff comes to the surface, patterns of behaviour and bad reactions that are buried deep in the sub-conscience come to the surface from our wounds of the past when life throws the stuff at us.
I believe that the meaning of suffering here is not referring to patiently accepting a lot of pain, but choosing to apply the new God given nature to your life instead of reacting in wayward living and living for your own pleasures as in the prodigal son.

This also means giving up our own religious thinking, self righteous acts, judging others how we perceive them as in the other brother.

Sometimes a person suffers from performance issues when they compare themselves to others and discover, they just aren't good enough, so they see themselves as inferior, give up and look for love and acceptance in the wrong places. Think about this possibility, the younger son growing up in the household, just doesn't do what is right and he tries to measure up as his older brother lives a model life in comparison, when the younger brother messes up he gets that look or some comments from older brother, get it right, get your act together.

How does he feel? Eventually he leaves in frustration, gets all the money he can, goes a long way off from the family, forgets about his failure to measure up.

The Prodigal Son lives a wild party lifestyle, here he is accepted as one of the crowd and has a good time, for a while.
This also can be a syndrome of certain misfits who just don't fit into society, they are the wrong type, colour, think differently, just a little crazy and loose, or they might not seem to have any talent at all apart from creating havoc, getting into strife in the process of trying to find their life skills.

There we have a possible background story for the prodigal son, can you relate to this, or you might know some that fit into this pattern.

We need to learn the choice of submitting our lives to God and allow His new life to ascend and rule our choices and life style.
Why submit? What is being humble really mean? For starters God has the best plan for our lives, knows us better than ourselves and His will is the best choice for our lives for our own good.
So, being humble is submitting to Gods will for our lives, giving up our will and what we think is best for our lives, especially since we have crooked thinking at times.
1 Peter 5:5
⁵ Likewise you younger people, submit yourselves to your elders. Yes, all of you be submissive to one another, and be clothed with humility, for "God resists the proud, but gives grace to the humble."
One of the biggest learning curves for the human race is to be submissive to others and submit to appropriate authorities appointed in our lives, as well as to Gods ways over our ways. There always just is a crooked thing that kicks in residing in each of us, when faced with choices to do the right thing.
1 Peter 5:6-10
⁶ Therefore humble yourselves under the mighty hand of God, that He may exalt you in due time,
⁷ casting all your care upon Him, for He cares for you.

We need to recognize that it is His resurrection power that raises us above the circumstances and trials of life.
Cast your cares upon Him for the solution.
[8] Be sober, be vigilant; because your adversary the devil walks about like a roaring lion, seeking whom he may devour.
[9] Resist him, steadfast in the faith, knowing that the same sufferings are experienced by your brotherhood in the world.
[10] But may the God of all grace, who called us to His eternal glory by Christ Jesus, after you have suffered a while, perfect, establish, strengthen, and settle you.

God cares for us and that says it all.
The Devil is on the lookout for access, where he can operate, he is powerless to function when the resurrection life of Jesus is present, rotten motives are removed by the purity of our Father in Heaven. Remember the devil is a defeated loser, so we don't have to give in to those hideous evil powers that can sway us to live a corrupt lifestyle. He only has the power if we let him have that control over us, he is the captain of the lost ship with stolen authority.

The enemy will look for a devious way in and it isn't when we are living in the lifestyle of Jesus. We need to draw from the wells of endless power over defeat, from the new life as a believer and partaker of the good things from the Father.

So, I don't think this refers to needless suffering from a ruthless attack from the enemy, or suffering the consequences of wrong choices away from a lifestyle of healthy living.

Take note: suffering and pain which leads to total destruction isn't from God, a refinement process for our betterment is, which is not the same, discernment needed, you can ask God. Humility is accepting Gods plan for our lives which leads to the abundance of life, otherwise going our own way is accepting Satan's plan for our lives, which leads to destruction.
We need to recognise what we are going through; whether it is an unauthorized assault of the enemy, or that we require wisdom for healthy lifestyle choices.

Suffering for the Kingdom of God can also come as persecution for our faith and we need the wisdom and strength of God to deal with each situation that comes across our path.

When our faith is tried and there is a refinement process in operation, where the heat is turned past the comfortable, this may also be a way of dealing with blockages and wrong attitudes and beliefs that are holding us back from being the better person as in the best design by God. Sometimes in His wisdom for our betterment, He is bringing us through an experience and process that will bring about change to be pure like Jesus is pure, being conformed into His image as a true son and daughter of God.

Let's not get confused by suffering and being held in bondage, by going through a loss that is not intended for us and missing out on the blessings of God.

Sickness and pain can be due to our poor choices or something generational coming through our bloodline and it isn't His will that we remain this way, as Jesus has already provided the victory, He purchased healing and wholeness by His stripes and our pains and wounds are restored to wholeness of a healthy, prosperous soul.

The enemy can't put suffering on you if you resist him and give the care to God. Receive His development, by humbling yourself and allow God to raise you up in the good life.

When the enemy came to Jesus he could find nothing to gain entry, there was no foothold of corruption, so he had to flee from Him and leave Him alone.

We are in the process of purification to become more like Him, to the place where we can no longer be devoured.

We can resist the enemy when we are in faith and stand on His promises knowing who we are as sons of God. We can be steadfast in the faith – faith in the power of resurrection life to raise us above being defeated by the limitations imposed by the fallen nature.

Look what happens after we go through the time of fire and trials that refine us to be a better person and our faith is made pure.

He builds in us 4 powerful life changing attributes in our process of change.
1. **Perfecting**
2. **Establishment**
3. **Strengthening**
4. **Settling**

These four attributes can be compared to the four (living creatures) found in the book of Revelation and these are in awe at the throne of God in Heaven.

The four living creatures consist of the face of a man and the face of a lion and the face of an ox and lastly the face of an eagle.

Four different characteristics can be represented here:-

Face of Man - Perfects us into the New Creation Man.

Face of a Lion- Establishes us into His Rule and Authority.

Face of an Ox - Strengthens us into His ability to overcome and stand firm.

Face of an Eagle - Settles us into a new position and perspective from above.

It is necessary for our development to go through the refining process in order that He can perfect, establish, strengthen and settle us into the new person that we are made to be in Christ. If we don't go through this process of refinement, as it is happening to all believers and it appears to be a very strange thing that we are going through, then the gold in us and our faith will not be perfected, but will remain a mixture of the dull old dross of what is part of our old habits which restricts our golden shine.

Let's humble ourselves and shine for Jesus, becoming the best person that we can be in this life and this is the best time to do this, we can't wait for Heaven, as then the opportunity to develop and be productive with His attributes in the Kingdom of God is past, it is better for us and others to shine His light in the darkness of this corrupted world to be part of His solution.
Don't you want those four fine attributes to occur now in this life, so that you can be more effective as a believer?
Consider the benefits of perfecting your weaknesses and establishing your ways into the image of Christ, then being strengthened in His grace and ability to endure, as well as being settled in the peace and knowledge from a whole new way of seeing things, way above our problems and troubles of this corrupt world.

Trials come to highlight what is not of faith and the weakness of our flesh and the dependencies of our old nature which tend towards independence from God.
When we humble ourselves acknowledging our weaknesses and dependency on the life of God to overcome, we will cast our cares on Him who is above.
We will be exalted with Him in our place of authority and rule over the many cares of this life.

Hab 2:4 ... "Behold the proud, his soul is not upright in him; but the just shall live by his faith."

There is pride resident in the carnal mind, this independent thinking will not humble itself under God, but lives itself in separation to purity and does what seems right, by looking out for the best interests of selfish desires.

The just are justified (just as if I – did not sin) they can live by faith in the power of resurrection life to be who God says they can be.

Our acceptance is not based on our past failures and weaknesses, whether we find ourselves afar off or even near to God. Discover the freedom that we are made in His image with a true identity fully accepted by the Father, with a unique gift to the world.

The parable named "the prodigal son" as told by Jesus is still relevant for us today, the focus being the dynamics between the two brothers.
In the parable there are disagreements leading to strife, which relates to the history of mankind, our individual world view and values can vary greatly, which leads to racial and political tensions that we see today in mixed global societies, which at the extreme level leads to violent hate crimes, progressing to wars and rumors of wars.
What social engineered policies will work and how can we stop human nature erupting during conflict?
How can there be peace when we are all so different in our individual makeup?

Globalism, Nationalism, Outbreaks of Terrorism, Religious Persecution based on Pride, signs of the changing times as we transition into the advancement of the human race in a post modern world, working for the plans of a sustainable, building of the utopian dream.

The flip side is that the Heavenly Father has made a way back for the lost sons and daughters to achieve their unique, individual greatness?

Is there a new creation reality for everyone and is the old nature of mankind history, when we put our faith in Jesus?
Is the other brother always going to be looking in disgust as his unworthy wayward brother is accepted back into the household?
Read on in the following chapters of *"Older Brother the Other"* you will see the bigger picture and hope for the tension between brothers in mankind.

We can all know the Fathers heart when we have fellowship with Him, we become one with His heart for others and our perspective will become the way of love.

The other brother can see that his brother the lost prodigal is a long way off.
He won't celebrate when he is accepted back and what was lost is found.
The Father celebrates to see His son be who he is made to be.

The Children of God

Copyright © March 2019

In this life our current stage of development is compared to children - it appears that is where we are at, primed and ready for growth and development as we go through the experiences of life and all that comes our way.

We are on a journey of discovery of who we really are – who am I really?

Growing up is developing into maturity, although our senses and perceptions are being trained by new experiences and challenges, this is the way we find our unique potential in the process of learning new things and doing life.
The 12 Disciples of Jesus who He especially chose, were limited and imperfect beings, but chosen for exceptional callings.

Enjoy Gods company and your Fathers affections, as He leads you and guides you on the way to development and growing up into Him and who you really are created to be. Nothing like being yourself with God's help.
He will not punish us for falling over and making mistakes, as like a child this is all part of the growing up and learning process. God the Father enjoys the process and will walk with us, holding our hand and smiles when we begin to try new things and learn by developing our senses and spiritual muscles, gaining in new found knowledge and understanding in a progressive way.

We tend to slip into one of the two following categories of the two sons portrayed in the prodigal son story.

Wasting our life potential in reckless pleasure indulgences in a self-lifestyle;
otherwise, living by performance in our own self-righteousness to gain approval and self-worth.
The nation of Israel famously tried to live their righteousness by the law.

Romans 9:30-32
30 What shall we say then? That Gentiles, who did not pursue righteousness, have attained to righteousness, even the righteousness of faith;
31 but Israel, pursuing the law of righteousness, has not attained to the law of righteousness.
32 Why? Because they did not seek it by faith, but as it were, by the works of the law.
For they stumbled at that stumbling stone.

We see a similar contrast between the brothers, on the one hand we have a person that did not live a good life, then turning around being restored and then we have the very zealous, religious person, that followed a set of rules to gain approval. This comparison correlates to the chosen Israelites who are in close vicinity to Gods principles and then the Gentiles who are outside the promised land doing their own thing, but later by faith are accepted into the family of God.

Now Israel did not enter into righteousness by faith but by their own works, which inevitably fell short and the Gentile when convicted and repented of their ways knowing full well that they did not measure up, entered into righteousness by faith.

Ephesians 2:11-13
11 Therefore remember that you, once Gentiles in the flesh—who are called Uncircumcision by what is called the Circumcision made in the flesh by hands—
12 that at that time you were without Christ, being aliens from the commonwealth of Israel and strangers from the covenants of promise, having no hope and without God in the world.
13 But now in Christ Jesus you who once were far off have been brought near by the blood of Christ.

Now notice the correlation that the Gentile or uncircumcised were excluded from the covenant of God initially and did not have any hope in their sinful state and where were they positioned? – afar off!!! Sound familiar?

Compare that to the prodigal and his position from the father in the story of the prodigal, in a similar way, he was far off and living a reckless life in sin.

However, is it the plan of God to leave us hopeless and without a way back to the Father?

By no means, God so loved the world that He sent His Son to bring even those afar off, accepted by the Blood of Jesus, which as you can see is a faith step back to God.

Now we all originally came from God as He created mankind in His image and before we entered this world our origins were in God, so there is a pull back to the beginnings again, to the original plan, which now is the rescue plan from our far off position. It is natural to be supernaturally reconnected to the Father by faith in Jesus.

What about Israel or the pious brother who lives by the rules, but is not applying faith, who does not enter into the Kingdom of God like a child who runs into the Fathers arms?

Ephesians 2:14-18
14 For He Himself is our peace, who has made both one, and has broken down the middle wall of separation,
15 having abolished in His flesh the enmity, that is, the law of commandments contained in ordinances, so as to create in Himself one new man from the two, thus making peace,
16 and that He might reconcile them both to God in one body through the cross, thereby putting to death the enmity.
17 And He came and preached peace to you who were afar off and to those who were near.
18 For through Him we both have access by one Spirit to the Father.

Once again the way to the Father is through the door of Jesus, He is the way the truth and the life and that is the Fathers desire to make peace and break down the barriers, against the one who is living far away from the ways of God and those that would be looked down upon by the religious sector.

The Father wants all to come to know Him and this means the religious one trying to keep the law, striving to reach perfection, which leads to judging others and judgement when the law is not kept to perfection, true freedom is found in the righteousness by faith in Jesus, who is the Saviour of the World.
Now this is the intention of God to create peace, reconciling the two, very different brothers, one who is far off in the things of God and one who is near to the laws and principles of God.
God no longer wants this distinction between the two brothers, that are so far apart in behaviour and responses to the law and religion. There is now peace and this is the peace of God that passes understanding, that is above what can ever be achieved in the natural.
Now God has made a new man created from the two, who are now one in Christ Jesus, they both will benefit from the diversities and differences in culture, personality and celebrate a whole new life that is complete and accepting of one another and be able to view others through the love of God.

God has created one new man who is one in Christ Jesus, the new creation lives by the blood of Jesus in resurrection lifestyle, living in the freedom of acceptance as a son or daughter of God, having the code written into their beings with divine power in their DNA, inherited from God the Father.

One new man made from the two.
Some mathematics out of this world
2=1 Two sons = one new man
3=2 Jesus and the 2 sons = Jesus and one new man

Well the real miracle is that He has created one new man and whether we are near to Him by trying to do the right thing or afar off by going our own way, we can now enter into the blessing of God and receive freely acceptance by the Father and live as the new man created in Christ Jesus.

How did the Father deal with each son?
First the Prodigal - all he wanted in the end was mercy and he came to the end of himself – been there and done it – now he just wanted to be back with the Father, not based on what he had done, just acceptance for who he can be – a son – undeserving, he did not demand anything like he did when he got his inheritance and wasted it on reckless living, now his attitude is asking for mercy and a new beginning.

The older brother was coming to the Father as – deserving of inheritance by living by the rules – he wasn't coming to the Father received as a son – the Father's desire is to give all good things to His children, but not from demanding children.

It is by relationship and love and yes He will forgive, when the son has strayed, when he chooses to return and come back under the ways of the Father, through learning a stiff lesson and losing it all, which is the trigger to rethink his position.

It is much easier when you know you blew it and you are afar off, to humble yourself before God and say, *"without you I am lost and can't make it on my own, I just waste it all and end up in the pig pen – please forgive me and receive me back and I will be your servant – much better to be a servant in God's house than seemingly having it all in a palace only to end up in reality eating pigs food."*

The other brother would find it hard to understand God's mercy, as he worked and earned it by the sweat of his brow and the prodigal does not deserve any special treatment.

The Self Righteous on their high horse look down on the under performers below, the other brother is relentless in his estimation of what the wayward brother deserves.

However, in the story of the prodigal son, we see that the father loves both sons and He says to the other brother, *"what I have is yours and you are always with me"*, that is what God wants, the sons and daughters to remain with Him and yes let's not pick on the other brother for trying to live in the right way and staying in the right place, that is commendable.

He just needed to adjust his attitude to one of seeing others through the eyes of love of the Father, not easy as the sinner's behaviour can be pitiful and someone who remains in that state without returning to the Father will remain in a pitiful state and without hope in this world.

No one needs to remain lost and far away, when it is a step of faith to turn back to the love of the Father and live in the new way of life that is free from the pig pen.

Yes I know there are varying degrees of sin and lifestyle and some would be near the middle of the road. No matter where you are in relation to God, you can't make it in by the sweat of your brow, trying to do the law and what is right in your own eyes, on the other hand you certainly are in a destructive place, remaining far off from God's ways.

We all just need to come on home and find the true love in the Fathers house.

One left home thinking there is another life somewhere else in the world, out there where anything goes, find yourself and get your own satisfaction.
Ended up feeding pigs, then going low down eating pig's food.
You know that your gift is wasted, living away from the Fathers house and is fed to the pigs, who have no real appreciation of your potential and well being and then you end up eating their trash to survive.

What is pig food?
Usually the left overs and the scraps, however, it is known that pigs eat just about anything and aren't discriminating in looking for what is healthy or nutritious and they also eat toxic waste and that is why in some places pork is not very hygienic, due to the waste products and dead bacteria infested by-products.

It has even being found that pigs eat rattlesnakes which are toxic and this is deposited in their meat, causing it to be toxic for human consumption, (this is not the case for all pork). Snakes are symbolic of demons, and cunning devices, devil's food, you don't want to go there. When we drift from the Fathers care it seems that the very food we eat becomes toxic as well, causing a decline in health and dumbing down, so we tend to end up passive and accepting of the trash and junkyard lifestyle and whatever is dished up to us in this state.

Usually when we are drawn into the temptations of the fast life there is offered all of the rich foods and delights, but as they say too much of a good thing is not good and over sweetened, sugar laden food is a nutrition killer; then when the money runs out as this lifestyle doesn't pay, it drains the resources, we end up on the cheap and nasty junk food, wasting us away. The enemy of our soul delights to have us in this passive dumbed down decline, so he can feed us with more of his trash.

We need to wake up and come to the end of ourselves, in the reckless self serving state, we hopefully will return to our senses and make our way back to the loving protection of the Father of our spirits and find a fulfilling life again.
God the Father keeps His loving eye on the prodigals and patiently waits for him or her to return.

The Other Brother thought his efforts alone will earn approval and a reward from the Father. Good behaviour will establish a person, but we are established towards completion on the Rock of what Jesus did for us and who He is and then doing His sayings in the faith of who we are created to be in the new creation reality.
I believe the answers to the main question will further lead us into a whole new dimension of questions and discovery to who we really are, but we really need to know what is our true identity and this is the journey of discovery.

Some food for thought, maybe a word puzzle, but keep searching and discovering your new horizons on the faith walk.

This is the dream and a knowing that we have from birth, however, sometimes life's traumas, may diminish this hope through abusive authority and voices, combined with other inherited, generational issues that flow through and bring a haze in our perceptions.
I was talking with a dying man and it came to me, as I perceived in his reflections and insight, that there is a place of great depth inside his being, as deep calls to deep, there is a well of salvation and the only way is to drop the bucket into the depths of our being, a place beyond the superficial, general knowledge and what our reasoning usually comprehends, this is the place where we may tap into, for the real answers.

We had this knowledge before we entered planet earth, when we in our beginnings as a spirit in the heavenlies, before time existed. Then we entered into a world of traumas; in this shocking transition, we gradually lost our innocence and that link to the spirit realm.
That is one of the reasons sickness occurs, because we are out of synch with who we are meant to be and our proper place of destiny, so our body reflects from our deep memories, a pain of not being right, which causes a restlessness which brings decay on the outward man.

God gave me, like a kick start in a life changing encounter which I had when I was a young teenager, He came into my natural existence and revealed the truth of another existence higher than my perceptions of reality, I discovered the Light of Life and the Lover of my soul and the peace of knowing and experiencing truth revealed. I still need to enter into this reality by faith and activate it, I can go where the light of life rises up and enters this plane of existence in the natural world of now and this is a process of learning, focusing on things above, where the real truth is and I have access to bring that into reality.

Colossians 3:1-3
1 If then you were raised with Christ, seek those things which are above, where Christ is, sitting at the right hand of God.
2 Set your mind on things above, not on things on the earth.
3 For you died, and your life is hidden with Christ in God.

Your real life is **hidden** with Christ and you need to discover it.

Colossians 3:10
10 and have put on the new man who is renewed in knowledge according to the image of Him who created him,

Peter Walked on the Water

Copyright © March 2019

When Peter kept his eyes on Jesus he walked on top of the water by faith.
When he looked at the wind and waves he sunk back into the sea of the natural elements, drawing him back down by the laws of gravity on the natural body.

Forces are at work that will pull us down into the self life, unless we keep our eyes on Him who saves us and keeps us above where we belong as sons with Him in the Heavenly Places.
When Peter looked at the wind and the waves, he sunk into the sea which was below where God wanted him to walk, the worldly forces and physical properties of gravity pulled him back down and under, out of faith and into natural ability.

Both the Prodigal and his resentful brother sunk back into the sea, as they both had their focus on themselves and what was around them and they both missed the mark of receiving their accepted identity of sons, freely given by the Father.

The Fathers acceptance was based on the inheritance freely provided to the Children of God, who benefit from the position of becoming a co-heir with Jesus, who is our way and our truth and our life.

We put on the new man by faith, stepping out of the boat, above the default position of the natural man, entering into the new dimension of the supernatural man, who is created into the new by faith in Christ Jesus.

Now the Sons and Daughters of God are enabled by steps of faith, with an excited Jesus calling us out of the adverse circumstances to walk on top of the waves and through the storm of the works of the enemy.

These hostile conditions are working against our success to bring us down into despair and discouragement, the storms are sent to try to dash us to pieces by the power of the adversities that comes against us, the enemy wants us to take our eyes off Jesus and forget who we really are in Christ in our naturally, stormy world.

When we rise above, by following the command of Jesus, we rise up out of the boat of familiarity and mediocrity and walk above the adversities and come into a whole new place of discovery in Him and find out the real – *"you can do it"*.

In the story of the Wizard of OZ there were three characters that along with Dorothy were on a pathway of discovery.
- *Tin Man – looking for a heart*
- *Straw man – needing a brain*
- *Lion Man – missing courage*

They all were on the journey looking for who they really were created to be.
They kind of knew they had the quality deep inside, but could not find the strength to have a real heart or have the real mind or have real courage, to be the person that they knew within, they had a glimmer of being.

We all have a God given destiny and this can be described as a *God Particle* that has uniquely gifted us, with the God kind of qualities that make a difference in this world.
Perhaps the wicked witch of the west has cast a vicious spell, or some other trauma has occurred, robbing our ability to find the true identity that we know we possess; it is within, we know it is there, but we just can't seem to express or release this gift, it has been somehow suppressed by adverse forces and we have slipped into a shell of a person and potential that we know is there, somewhere.

So, we carry on in the world, however, the same old syndrome grips us when confronted by the daunting tests, where we collapse within and just can't seem to find that quality to rise above. Instead a pathetic shadow surfaces and that is all we can muster on our day of battle, fear and doubt take their insidious grip, reinforcing the hopeless image of the loser embedded within our psyche; it overwhelms that faint hope of what our potential should be and the witches and naysayers speak loud with sick reminders **"loser!"**
Now along the way on our journey of life to find our true identity, we have the hopes of reaching the potential of our best dreams and desires, we inevitably meet others who are searching, just like we are and have their own issues to deal with.

This is the time when we are offered a wizard of a solution, a magical way to be made whole, we live in hope of the wizard of OZ who magically can fix all of our deficits, as he is truly amazing. When we finally meet him with great expectations and trusting in the abilities of this acclaimed, miracle worker, we eventually come to the disappointing revelation, that he is just a little man with a loud voice.

Despair sets in, as once again we have been let down by false hopes of a cure and we see that when limited mankind as great as he can be, offers the cure, it turns out to be just a loud voice projected with lots of props, bells and whistles but, no life changing, permanent substance.

Well the truth is that we need to go to God, who has given to us the God type of life - particle and there is no magic recipe from a special person that will cure us with a lot of wizardry. All created beings are like little peas, compared to the vastness and splendour of God, despite all of man's amazing technology and inventions with ever increasing knowledge, projected all over the world, there is God who created all and He alone made all of us in His unique design.
The potential planted in each of us is a unique, God design DNA, that we all have been given, we just need to unlock all of its mysteries and fulfill it in this life.

Ending up with a bunch of other losers, wandering along in life with a dreamy young lady full of songs, headed to a place where some magic will be performed by a wizard, who really just is a small man with a very good PR marketing program, that projects his message globally on the super highway of information, sadly this is not the answer. Are you aware that you are uniquely made, with an individual potential to rock the world like no one else could ever do or be!

Are you are missing the heart to perform it, lacking the mind to comprehend it and the courage to face all of the opposition and wicked voices and stand up for yourself and finally overcome?

How can we find the missing attribute and the essence of who we really are in the storms and adversities of life?
Change and power – *spirit soul and body – heart, mind and courage (body)*
The truth is; this is the plan of God for his children; that we are conformed to the image of the new man, our complete brother Jesus and to reflect the mystery of Christ in us.

His plan is to bring back the wayward and the lost of the prodigals, far away sons back into His arms, into the ways of right, life choices.
Then He also wants to liberate the other brother to receive the love that surpasses knowledge that conforms him, into a destiny that is walking with the Father, that is vibrant and fun as well as being a productive member for the Kingdom of God.

He makes one new man from the two – one is a far off from living right – the other is near to the ways of God, but hasn't entered into the newness of a close relationship with the Father in the freedom of the new creation man.

The God Particle

Have you got it?

Copyright © March 2019

Everyone has a God Particle as we are all created individual, distinct, but contain a unique blend of DNA that is divine and original and delightfully ingenious.

Everyone is unique in design and we are made in His image with a God Particle that makes us like the snowflake individual, fearfully and wonderfully made.

***Psalm 139:14**
14 **I will praise You, for I am fearfully** **and wonderfully made;**
Marvelous are Your works,
And that my soul knows very well.

This gives each individual a distinct advantage, a gift and potential and there is no other like it; each one has been given an individually tailored expression from the God particle that makes us who we really are.

However, along with all of this wonderful potential and supreme uniqueness comes a disadvantage, or better put, there is a lack in this uniqueness. There is a need for one God particle that is extremely gifted like no other, but this is limited as marvelous as each one is to the scope, of the potential given.

Therefore, there is a need for other God particles to become a complete unit, as together we all make up a whole, this becomes a united, integrated strength, collaboratively, we work together and express and supply our gift and receive from others their individual gift, that makes each one an integral part of the body of workmanship, connected to the Head who is Jesus our Lord and King.

Ephesians 4:7, 8
7 But to each one of us grace was given according to the measure of Christ's gift.
8 Therefore He says:
"When He ascended on high,
He led captivity captive,
And gave gifts to men."
So, here it is, the grace gifting that has been given to all who enter into Christ as the new, gifted person in Him.

We all are unique and have received our own individual calling and the grace gift that Jesus in His eternal wisdom knows exactly what is the best fit for everyone.

No one else can do the gift like you or I can, we all need each other to shine in our gifts and benefit from the God particle within.
Ephesians 4:9, 10
9 (Now this, "He ascended"—what does it mean but that He also first descended into the lower parts of the earth?
10 He who descended is also the One who ascended far above all the heavens, that He might fill all things.)
Why did He need to descend first?
This is a transaction, a ledger written, where there is a credit and a debit and a balancing of the books, as God is a God of justice. Jesus descended on our behalf and went where we deserved to go, with our sins and weaknesses to deposit them and pay for them in full.
Then He was raised up in righteousness in faith, of the promise of the Father.
He had taken our punishment once and for all, no one no matter how evil, or no power could ever hold Him down.
He rose again and this is also for our benefit, as we enter into the other side of the transaction, where grace will provide a new life in Him to walk in the gifting's that He has provided and we appropriate His righteousness, to develop character that compliments the gift, a faith expression in love.

When He descended, He took our weaknesses of the long way off and the near, but not connected and all of the iniquities that create patterns of failure in our lives and then He rose again, ascended, victorious in Resurrection power to provide us with victory and an ability to overcome all of the weaknesses that we have and that could potentially take us down and away from God.
He ascended and was then able to give gifts to men, to distribute and be a blessing to others to help them also overcome and become Christ like, in whatever grace gift He gave to each one, all have an essential part to provide nourishment and help in our particular forte, that helps us and others to be overcomers and therefore, each one is gifted uniquely and is a part of the overall answer and we all need to learn to acknowledge each other's unique gift and submit to one another, as He has given each one an authority to administer resurrection life for the benefit of the body and those being added.

A God particle expression is given for you and for me.

Ephesians 4:11-15
11 And He Himself gave some to be apostles, some prophets, some evangelists, and some pastors and teachers,
12 for the equipping of the saints for the work of ministry, for the edifying of the body of Christ,

13 till we all come to the unity of the faith and of the knowledge of the Son of God, to a perfect man, to the measure of the stature of the fullness of Christ;
14 that we should no longer be children, tossed to and fro and carried about with every wind of doctrine, by the trickery of men, in the cunning craftiness of deceitful plotting,
15 but, speaking the truth in love, may grow up in all things into Him who is the head— Christ—

This is important to note, that we all grow into the fullness and maturity of Christ and the various gifts in the body of Christ, all have a crucial role to help equip others for their ministry and help all to grow up into Him. It is not a superman or superwoman who has some powerful gift that we focus on, all of the gifts and the greater works point us towards Jesus alone. The key is that all remain connected to the Head who is Jesus and receive through Him by the Spirit of God, working together in His submitted Body of Believers.

Ephesians 4:16
16 from whom the whole body, joined and knit together by what every joint supplies, according to the effective working by which every part does its share, causes growth of the body for the edifying of itself in love.

Now you see the benefits that each one of us possess as a gift and calling to complement each other and make up the Body of Christ in completion, to be His expression on earth and see His will be done here and His Kingdom come here, right where we live, in our unique time and place of our destiny, as we supply our part.

This is really talking about alignment, the body of Christ needs to come into alignment to function properly, where each part will be connected in the appropriate place, to be nourishment and receive energy and the life of the body where each part is made to fit as an effective member that is not disconnected or maligned. This means there is a right place for all in the overall body of Christ to fit and to function.

If you are feeling out of place, or you are like a round peg forced into a square, check and wait on God for your solution and placement, He will direct your paths. Don't expect perfection even when in the right place, there will be a refinement towards maturity, as each one is developed and the weak muscles strengthened and the toxins removed.

THE TEMPLE

Copyright © Feb 2025

1 Corinthians 6:19-20
19 Or do you not know that your body is the temple of the Holy Spirit who is in you, whom you have from God, and you are not your own?
20 For you were bought at a price; therefore glorify God in your body and in your spirit, which are God's.
Ephesians 2:20-22
20 having been built on the foundation of the apostles and prophets, Jesus Christ Himself being the chief cornerstone,
21 in whom the whole building, being fitted together, grows into a holy temple in the Lord,
22 in whom you also are being built together for a dwelling place of God in the Spirit.

A future vision, as well as some history.

Once again there is a fitting together of all members in the body of Christ, we all have a place and are connected into the overall plan and intention of our Head who is Jesus. There is the individual and there is the overall body as a temple, where God now dwells. This is what Church really is, a chosen people who have accepted God and allowed His Spirit to enter in and make them into a place of prayer, a connection and love relationship between man and God where God now lives and rules.

There are three temples mentioned in the bible and two of those have already existed but were destroyed in history, the other is mentioned but not built yet.

We can make a comparison to those actual Jewish structures to the body or temple of man.

First - there is the fall of man which is compared to the first temple built by the wisdom of Solomon, this glorious temple was knocked down by the *Babylonians*, led by *Nebuchadnezzar*, who reigned over all of mankind.

Second - came the collapse of the chosen Jewish nation, from where came the commandments and ordinances of Moses, this temple was destroyed by the *Roman Empire* who established the ruling civilization of mankind.

Seasons of change in history are necessary to bring us forward into the new man and our highest calling,
as there was a shift in the religious, cultural, political, and economical atmosphere and with each shift came a removal of the old structures of society to usher in the new.

Now I have likened the temple to three phases in the spiritual development and changes of mankind as each critical event occurred to usher in major changes, the old system was removed, ushering in the new age, making way for the new structure and the new spiritual dimension of a whole new man.

1st Temple - Adam.
2nd Temple - Moses.
3rd Temple - Jesus.

1st temple was taken out by Adam and Eve falling into the original temptation, when they ate the forbidden fruit from the *Tree of Knowledge of Good and Evil*
(pleasant to the eyes and tastes good) but made man separate from God and removed the original state of innocence *(a bit like when we were in the innocence of our youth)*.

When our eyes are open to the possibility of knowing what is evil, we are offered the choice and man could not resist its power to corrupt, as only God and those who have being perfected in Him can overcome these temptations.

2nd temple was taken out by the Spirit of Religion, which is self orientated and inward looking for the discovery of the powers of man within, unlocked potential in the regions of the soul, this created a structure of self knowledge, which makes a self set of rules, knowing good and evil to make a self-set of commandments which forms the traditions of man.
Also, the fruit of the *Tree of Knowledge of Good and Evil - (appeals to the soul, where we are at the centre of our universe in control)*.

3rd temple will be perfected by God as we grow in maturity into the one new man in Him, the new Creation Man that He predestined for us to enter into and be complete as the manifested mature Sons of God. The proposed physical temple is yet to be fulfilled historically, as the temple structure has not been built, the site of the temple is in Jerusalem.

It is important to observe who builds and eventually occupies the new temple. Real or counterfeit? Let the reader understand! The future will reveal the outcome and the true nature of this final temple structure, when the ascendancy of mankind will rise on forces only to be later destroyed, as there is no completion and only ultimate corruption when the body is filled by the wrong force from the dark source.

Prophetically, we understand that there will be a completion in the temple of man by God, his body on earth represented by the overall body of Christ will be transformed, into the completion of the maturity of the sons manifested on earth in completeness of the one new man in Christ.

This may be in fullness when the return of Christ occurs, or in the peak of a mature son and daughter and spotless bride of Christ, this side of the completion and the coming change from mortal to immortal and having a perfect body. God only knows or has He revealed this to His prophets.

The physical temple referred to is most likely based on the plans given to the prophet Ezekiel for this coming 3rd temple which will be constructed in Jerusalem in Israel, *(all eyes on Jerusalem - look for the signs)* as at the moment this is a contentious site for this majestic construction.

At this critical juncture of the apex of man in the upwards triangle of advancement, we either succumb to the next deception of the fruit of the *Tree of Knowledge of Good and Evil*, which is *"you will be like gods"* and in this enticement is deception, which is a lie mixed with a truth.

The truth is that we may become like Christ, when we are conformed to His image and the likeness of His resurrection from the dead.

If we choose to submit ourselves to the process of change and discovery of the new man, then we will enter into the blessings and full inheritance that the Father has planned for us at the end of the age and I believe we will see a progression in the Body of Christ in the coming days, which is known as the end times.
The Glory of God will be revealed in all sorts of demonstrations of miracles, signs and wonders to further the Kingdom of God on earth and be blessings and deliverance to mankind with the ushering in of a great end time harvest of souls, this will occur amongst chaos and calamity on the earth, but the Light of the Good News of Jesus Christ will shine the brightest; receive this eternal blessing and never ending love of Father God.

However, if we don't receive the message of the Good News, then we will fall to the ultimate deception away from the truth of being conformed to the image of Christ, to becoming a *god in our own eyes*, by the flattery of a delusion of the counterfeit greatness which is independent from God the Father, who is the I AM and the only true source of life.
Now we all don't want to go on the path of deception, we really want the fruit of the Tree of Life which now is available to us, who believe in Jesus and receive His life to grow us into the new man of our true uncorrupted identity.

The Collective Consciousness of Mankind

Copyright © March 2019

What if we all combined our thinking and our best abilities and together, mankind could work together for the common good.

Sounds like a Post Modernist vision of Utopia, as we face the imbalances due to disproportionate accumulation and domination of the wealth by the elite, mass food production leading to depleted nutrition and GM foods, along with pharmaceuticals pills that try to patch us up from the effects of our modern society that stresses most people out, alienates us and slows us down mentally, so we just struggle to exist, looking for the meaning of it all and trying to get some highs somehow on the weekends.

These are restless times as the world systems go into decline, with failing economies, unprecedented failing countries bank accounts, declining currencies and population issues, where there are shortages of food and commodities and climate pollution and then there are wars and terrorist troubles and uprisings of civil unrest, disturbing violent protests raging with disapproval of the present ruling governments and the ruling powers who control the resources and wealth.
So we need a solution, we need to be progressive and revolutionary in our thinking to deal with the current catastrophic declines in our world.

In Genesis 11 we read about the Tower of Babel, how mankind combined forces and constructed a mighty city and a tower reaching to the heavens.
Genesis 11:4-6
4 And they said, "Come, let us build ourselves a city, and a tower whose top is in the heavens; let us make a name for ourselves, lest we be scattered abroad over the face of the whole earth."
5 But the Lord came down to see the city and the tower which the sons of men had built.
6 And the Lord said, "Indeed the people are one and they all have one language, and this is what they begin to do; now nothing that they propose to do will be withheld from them.

The people were one and had one language,
they were going to make a name for themselves
and it was observed that, in this collective mind,
they could do whatever they propose;
a doorway was opened to the realms of
advanced possibilities.

Would not this be a good thing? After all God
said to Adam go and have dominion on the
earth?

So what is the problem?
Man c'mon!

Fast forward to today where our languages are
different and there are many nationalities and
different cultures, religions etc.
How would you combine these?
We have the technology!

Technology is advancing at ultimate light speeds,
atomic particles discovered taking knowledge
beyond the traditional.

The internet is such a technology that makes one
big, world wide network and this is where minds
can connect from all over the world and it is
possible to translate languages using digital
interpretations.

Again, what is wrong with that? It is a good thing to open up knowledge and make connections world wide and as we have seen, this accelerates knowledge exponentially and imaginations can conceive all sorts of possibilities and there is talk of time travel, transportation like on star trek where we are beamed up, well we have a brave new world in the making and society will reach new heights that we dream about and see on the movies and futuristic novels and the imaginations of thinking men of tomorrow.

Daniel 12:4
4 But thou, O Daniel, shut up the words, and seal the book, even to the time of the end: many shall run to and fro, and knowledge shall be increased.

Daniel got a glimpse into the future, at the time of the end and saw knowledge increased and a running about and movement, to and fro.
He also saw the antichrist that arose to rule the nations.

Google wants to collect all information and make a super, monster database that will map a world of possibilities.
Google policy is *"do no evil!"*
There is a lot of talk about the implanted micro chip into the hand or forehead that will be used to store information and possibly link us to the banking system and governing agencies.
The following is a *what if* scenario – just kind of throwing it out there.

I acknowledge information and findings of end time teachers and activists with a bit of the conspiracy thrown in, none dare call it a conspiracy and big brother, these and my own revelations, which has form the basis for the following end time scenario.

What if in our advanced technology, this chip also had the ability to connect us by our mind and thinking to the internet and then create a collective consciousness?
We have already seen that they have technology where a person is wired up and can think commands to the computer, or cause mechanical limbs to move.
Now each human being is unique and has a unique frequency that no other has, so think about that, like a MAC address or an IP address if you like and through our unique identifier and a chip that has access to the internet, bingo we are now connected with the beast, or the ultimate global server, to be part of a world wide new system of collective thinking.

There is talk also, that there is technology to transmit thoughts and suggestions, so that we are like sleepers, triggered at some point by an agency, this is possible as we are located by our own unique frequency and then the perpetrator may implant suggestions and thinking in our mind and this would be a violation of an unauthorized entry into our minds.

Now the way of the future is wireless connectivity and therefore, we like portable devices such as cell phones and are connected wherever we roam.

Think of the benefits, there would be health monitoring and regulation, the chip could identify health issues or corrections that we need, connect to the internet database and add the required patches, who knows it may have some internal abilities that can be transmitted to our minds or adjust something in our DNA to fix potential detected viruses and problems. Learning would be easy, beam up the schematics and the how to, into our thoughts and there you are, solved - downloaded. When connected to super computers and other minds, you now have the advantage of collective resources and applications. The possibilities are endless and all of those movies like *minority report* can be reality, where corrective thinking can be made to aggression or negative attitudes, as this is all monitored by our friendly and helpful BIG BROTHER.

C'mon get with the program!

It is for the common great good of mankind, you are not going to go religious and fundamental on us? Why not accept what the great thinktanks are saying and the ever progressive elite, who are a class above and they want what is best for everyone. Yeh right!

Think about when something inside you breaks down, they can detect it on the mankind monitoring system and pull you back into the mothership for some much needed modifications and bingo! Like new, send you out again like a new man, all fixed up and society friendly, no radical fringe, suspicious potentially bi-polar, swing to the negative that has to be stopped, before you become a ticking time bomb infecting the correctness instilled into the global population.

Sci Fi, Freaky, out there and wild whacky – we may do whatever we propose!
So we may believe, but this would be the ultimate deception of the counterfeit.

That is brave new world and the matrix combined forces to create a what?

One New Man!!!

What is the number of man? 6
It will be the beast.
What is missing from 6?
The one who makes it 7.

Copyright © March 2025

Back to the old fallen mankind disconnection again and independence from God who created us and is the true source of what is good and is life.
With God man who is 6 becomes ultimately 7 which is perfected.
We are talking about end times here and the future is upon us, right at the door, we are looking at massive changes on the global futuristic world scene.

At the tower of Babel, they were going to reach the heights in the heavens, in a combined, collective mind of mankind, to make a name for themselves.
The ultimate achievement of mankind *Spirit Soul Body 666.*
We could have a new man created, but void of God.

There would be no Christ in us, shameful, what would there be if there is a vacuum? What would replace the void?
Matthew 24:15
15 *"Therefore when you see the 'abomination of desolation,'spoken of by Daniel the prophet, standing in the holy place"*
(whoever reads, let him understand)
2 Thessalonians 2:3, 4
3 *Let no one deceive you by any means; for that Day will not come unless the falling away comes first, and the man of sin is revealed, the son of perdition,*
4 *who opposes and exalts himself above all that is called God or that is worshiped, so that he sits as God in the temple of God, showing himself that he is God.*
When you take out God from your life, you have a void, this is filled with something else which is a force, like when light is removed you have darkness.
The 3rd temple well may be actual and physical, it will be a place of contention as to who is going to rule and possess it.

Our bodies are described as temples as well as a type of the actual, now the real temple is in Heaven and the one on earth is a copy, but we are types of a place where the presence of God dwells and there are ceremonies and proceedings and a progression through the temple into the inner regions.

Our bodies are a place where we are meant to invite the Spirit of God to dwell and occupy as a completion from a 6 to a 7 - being perfected, Christ in us.
However when you don't make that choice, ultimately, another force opposite of positive, an unclean spirit of darkness will possess or occupy. The revelation of the temples illustrates the progression of mankind spiritually, firstly the Sin of Adam took mankind afar off and then the Law of Moses brought the chosen race Israel near, then finally, perfection, the 3rd temple, where the new man is created from the two.

There are two ways we can go in the new man, a temple filled with the glory of God, or a brave new matrix, world, a temple filled with a mystery 666? The 666 creation is the pinnacle of mankind without God, an obelisk of the brave new man. The next fascinating observation in relation to these developments is in
I John 2:15-17
15 Do not love the world or the things in the world. If anyone loves the world, the love of the Father is not in him.

*16 **For all that is in the world—the lust of the flesh, the lust of the eyes, and the pride of life—is not of the Father but is of the world. 17 And the world is passing away, and the lust of it; but he who does the will of God abides forever.***

- *Lust of the flesh*
- *Lust of the eyes*
- *Pride of Life*

3 areas:
Body Soul Spirit
Resulting in the marring effect of sin:-
Body – appearance
Soul – personality and thinking
Spirit – belief

Lust of the flesh – health
Lust of the eyes – perception
Pride of life – motivations

We see historically and currently, the effect of sin on mankind, which distorts beauty and brings destruction in ugly fashion and this is not due to a God who wants to inflict punishment as portrayed by false reports, as men need to choose whether they remain in the family of their true origin, or move far away from the house of God and place themselves outside the protection and the favour provided, as a position of choice, we subject ourselves to adverse consequences and it isn't Gods will that we stray into trouble.

So, do you now believe the hideous lie that God is taking away our fun and freedom? This is an outrageous lie from the pits, to misrepresent God and take away our trust in Him. Instead we need to see the truth that He loves us and does not want anyone to be harmed or fall into destruction; He is instructing us for our own good.

Like a father who sees his child moving towards deadly, fast moving traffic, he gives a loud command and warning and will grab their tiny hand, the father would be devastated to see his child ignore the call and wander off into danger. Now this depends on the age and development of the child as to how the father instructs him, or what he can do in a situation of impending danger.
Is the child a grown up able to make his own choices? The father will still want to reason with him, is he a teenager and listening to a bunch of friends saying "come on it is fun to play with danger, live fast!"
Or a toddler running fast, but unaware where he is going? All different stages and then there are different personalities, whatever the case, the father will do his best to rescue the child, even if it means yelling at him or what – God forbid a smack!
Is yelling hostile and insensitive to a person's feelings and then horrors is a paddy whack barbaric? What are the demands and the action required to remedy the alarming situation? Let us reason together!

Whoops sorry, controversial!
Discipline in love is the cure, discipline in a rage is damaging to children.
Put yourself in the situation as the father and what would you do when you see your beloved child walking, or running towards danger!!!

Now I don't believe that the children in heaven would be physically smacked by the Father in heaven, all of the accounts I have heard do not suggest that there are angels smacking naughty children in heaven. The children in heaven are under developed and are still maturing, but their spirit is alive and their perceptions are heightened and they don't have rebellion bound up in their nature.
On earth, we need to take crude measures to deal with the crude atmosphere where rebellion is in the heart of children and sadly in an imperfect world, we need to take measures to deal with the issues that are here. Unfortunately it does mean that the only way a rebellious, stubborn person will respond and perhaps stop and listen to sound advice is when they are administered, disciplinary action.
This doesn't mean that God is the author of sickness and pain, no there is a demented being called Satan, who is bent on dishing out whatever torture is at his disposal on human beings as his warped idea of dealing with humans, so when we persistently and knowingly rebel, we willingly move out of the place of protection into a place where that lunatic will do harm to us.

If we persistently refuse to accept God's love and warnings then we will enter into what is known as punishment, or the consequences of freedom of choice given to all.
In a different way there is what is known as discipline, which actually is administered for our good, it may seem painful at the time, but will rescue us from suffering and torment from the maniac killer, the devil and his psycho hordes.

Now I can say by experience that God is longsuffering and merciful and will persist with us, in the hope of seeing us come to our senses and return to His loving arms.
In the following versus it is revealed that there is deception in this world, particularly in relation to the end times, which we are now living in, it is very relevant for us to be aware of the devices at work to deceive.

I John 2:18-19
18 Little children, it is the last hour; and as you have heard that the Antichrist is coming, even now many antichrists have come, by which we know that it is the last hour.
19 They went out from us, but they were not of us; for if they had been of us, they would have continued with us; but they went out that they might be made manifest, that none of them were of us.

So, if we don't continue in the process of the truth to discover the new man of Christ in us, our hope of Glory, we will slip into the deception of being a god in in our own grand delusion, a false belief that without God we can make it and be somebody, the reality is we are somebody connected to the Antichrist.

I John 2:20-21
20 But you have an anointing from the Holy One, and you know all things.
21 I have not written to you because you do not know the truth, but because you know it, and that no lie is of the truth.
We need to remain in the truth and not stray away, there is an entertaining lie dished up to take our fancy.
I John 2:22-23
22 Who is a liar but he who denies that Jesus is the Christ? He is antichrist who denies the Father and the Son.
23 Whoever denies the Son does not have the Father either; he who acknowledges the Son has the Father also.

Now we see that we need to be connected to God the Father and Jesus His Son to become the new man and His Spirit now lives in us, to assist us in every way.
I John 2:24-27
24 Therefore let that abide in you which you heard from the beginning. If what you heard from the beginning abides in you, you also will abide in the Son and in the Father.

25 And this is the promise that He has promised us—eternal life.
26 These things I have written to you concerning those who try to deceive you.
27 But the anointing which you have received from Him abides in you, and you do not need that anyone teach you; but as the same anointing teaches you concerning all things, and is true, and is not a lie, and just as it has taught you, you will abide in Him.

There are those that are blinded by a demented ego of over inflated self importance, they will tell you with gross flattery, that you can become great and be like a god, but they don't tell you that you will become like the god of this world, who is obscenely degenerated and driven by lust, to kill, steal and destroy our true identity.

We have an anointing that alerts us to the lie and keeps us, as we remain in the ways of the Father and His Kingdom within.

2019 commentary on conspiracy theories.

I have proposed a possible scenario mentioned in the previous collective consciousness of mankind chapter from insights given and my investigations from the various influences found out there on Cyber Space. However, I would like to add that this is a proposed scenario only, what actually eventuates precisely is unknown, this scenario may form a part of the puzzle, time will tell how the end times antichrist global system is devised and the technologies combined with dark spiritual forces is used by the master minded enemy of mankind. I can tell you that Satan is a vastly superior intelligent being and yes his motivations are dark and twisted, but he is not silly, foolish for rebelling against God, of cause. In other words the enemy is not predictable, he knows what is put out there on the internet and knows how to use Google if he needs to.

Therefore, if a conspiracy theory is widely circulated already, you can bet your bottom dollar that it is already been scrapped for an even more devious plan, within his ongoing dark intentions, he has multiple scenarios that may play out and be abandoned at a drop of a hat, replaced by the chosen plan from multiple cunning options. Satan has moved on and by hook and by crook, he will shift to the best available plan at the permitted time.

What is brought to light by the watchmen however, will correctly reveal elements of how the enemy may create a global new world order domination that controls the masses with the mark of the beast, blinding the captives by this sinister technology combined with dark forces into a world wide system accompanied by lying signs and wonders. He can shift and switch like a slithering snake in the grass waiting for its prey, maneuvering skillfully with expert observation and the schemes remain hidden, until the cunning snake strikes at the optimum time, times and half a time.

We won't know fully unless the Holy Spirit reveals, but we can foil many plans by bringing these intentions to light.
Another divisive strategy by the enemy is a smoke screen, diverting attention and people's perceptions to distrust and distance themselves from what is true. The enemy makes use of the extreme crimes committed, by the far right groups who are motivated by hate. This image can be painted onto what is perceived by association, the Christians who are perceived to be right wing, labelled and grouped with this side of the fence. Tarred with the same brush is the narrative painted all over those with Christian beliefs.
Judgements are made.
The verdict is out.
With the same brush stained.

There are other ways of seeing things, think of combining left and right together as another state. Like 0 and 1 and then 01 combined or superimposed together as another position. This one new combined state takes on the best of both sides of the equation, creating a new perspective. No extremes, just a cool fusion. From a faith perspective, there is a higher law operating that brings two different sides together and creates a perfect union, Jesus has made ONE from the two. Jesus is neither, a conservative, or a liberal, left or right wing, He is the perfect combination of both and infinitely more.

Therefore, speaking the truth in love without compromising values, is how this works.

God bless you and enlighten you by His Holy Spirit who leads us into all truth and shows us things to come, He is our wise counsellor that can reveal things above what we can normally conceive or interpret.

Little Children

Copyright © March 2025

The Apostle John refers to us as little children; let's take another look at this.
What does that say about our development level?

Let's just say that as we begin the journey of life, that this is the first stage of the ages that we will live forever in, we can be assured that we are just beginning to learn from the wisdom and knowledge of God.

John also says what a privilege it is to be called sons and daughters of God.

That is what we are, believe me God loves us with a Fathers love, He lovingly watches our progression in life and as we know as parents, children are learning and they make mistakes and have many attempts to gain new understanding and we know this is a natural development. So it is in the spiritual, God isn't there with a big stick when we miss it in the spirit!

So when we aren't quite in the zone with our asking and using our authority that is OK, we are in the learning stages and need to keep on going as God is watching with a smile.
Also, you will notice that children can be quite demanding at times, and can throw tantrums, when they don't get what they want! Been there! Well the parent can deal with that and still loves the child, but needs to be firm and say no at times, for the best interests of the child. Asking for things that are excessive or unhealthy and many other valid examples, it is similar in the spirit, we don't always ask for the right thing and we are learning and need to trust, that the Father of our spirits will guide us into maturity and He won't give us anything that will be harmful, He is the giver of good gifts, so enjoy your development as God is enjoying that you are part of His eternal family on His track of life forevermore in abundance and don't worry, you won't miss out on the best.

Ephesians 1:5, 6
5 having predestined us to adoption as sons by Jesus Christ to Himself, according to the good pleasure of His will,
6 to the praise of the glory of His grace, by which He made us accepted in the Beloved.
It is Gods good pleasure to accept us as sons and daughters and to be part of His family, He just wants to gather us up in His huge, loving arms. It truly is His grace, His never ending love, that we are accepted by what Jesus purchased for us to be with Him forever.

Accountability – Righteousness Living.
There is always going to be excess as long as we remain like a child before the sons of God are manifested who will display the maturity of Christ in them.
You give the flesh an inch it will take a mile!
Can I relate to this? Regrettably yes, I have been slack at times and loose in character, the old *I want* rises up and takes the opportunity to gain mastery of the soul, they call it 2nd nature, it is just there waiting – our dark shadow does not go away until the final curtain at the return and brightness of our Lord and our King Jesus.
So when we are struggling with sin, condemnation is not good, but conviction is OK, as the Holy Spirit who lives in us is sent to counsel us and He will point out where we are in error, alerting us from straying away from being in Christ.

So Grace is not a license to sin!!!

Hyper means excess and when you have too much sugar going through your blood this is not healthy. However, in this case the problem is not getting too much grace, but digesting an impure interpretation of what grace means – so like sugar it tastes sweet, but it is poison to the health of the body.
I am sure you know what I mean; let the Holy Spirit guide you into all truth.

Conviction leads us to the answer in Christ, where as condemnation leads us away from the answer, telling us there is no hope and we end up in despair.
Romans 13:8-14
8 Owe no one anything except to love one another, for he who loves another has fulfilled the law.
9 For the commandments, "You shall not commit adultery," "You shall not murder," "You shall not steal," "You shall not bear false witness," "You shall not covet," and if there is any other commandment, are all summed up in this saying, namely, "You shall love your neighbor as yourself."
10 Love does no harm to a neighbor; therefore love is the fulfillment of the law.
11 And do this, knowing the time, that now it is high time to awake out of sleep; for now our salvation is nearer than when we first believed.
12 The night is far spent, the day is at hand. Therefore let us cast off the works of darkness, and let us put on the armor of light.

**13 Let us walk properly, as in the day, not in revelry and drunkenness, not in lewdness and lust, not in strife and envy.
14 But put on the Lord Jesus Christ, and make no provision for the flesh, to fulfill its lusts.**
God isn't extending some kind of free sin ticket called grace for those that continually disregard the law, in a life of rebellion and particularly, those that intentionally do others harm.
Do what thou wilt is not grace. Do *Christ in you* is grace, as that has to be some sort of gift to be as He is.

There is a sword and God given authority on earth in the arm of justice in police and authorities that at some point, will take effect and deal with lawlessness.
Notice now that Christ has come and opened up the veil for us to enter into and see a better Covenant, there is a focus on the love of God which now motivates us to do the right thing and empowers us to be in obedience to the requirements of the law, as Jesus came to fulfill the law and provide us the freedom in the New Creation Man to enter into and to be like Christ our Righteousness.

Why is it now closer to the time than when we first believed?
Surely when I believed I was saved, so I have my salvation?

What is Salvation in this context?
It is completeness and healing and restoration to how things were meant to be. Jesus has died on the cross and opened the door to a realm of resurrection life and now we are closer to the day where this will be completed. The sons and daughters of God will be manifest and reach maturity and as we draw nearer to His return, the closer we are to the possibility of living in completeness. As now we have entered into His fullness and we are partakers of His divine abilities, so we need to awake from the passiveness of allowing the old nature to rule and awake to entering into His promises by faith.

Hebrews 4:1, 2

Therefore, since a promise remains of entering His rest, let us fear lest any of you seem to have come short of it.

2 For indeed the gospel was preached to us as well as to them; but the word which they heard did not profit them, not being mixed with faith in those who heard it.

This is a call to enter into the position of rest in the promise of the new man in Christ and remain in the faith and blessings.

Hebrews 4:11-13

11 Let us therefore be diligent to enter that rest, lest anyone fall according to the same example of disobedience.

12 For the word of God is living and powerful, and sharper than any two-edged sword, piercing even to the division of soul and spirit, and of joints and marrow, and is a discerner of the thoughts and intents of the heart.

13 And there is no creature hidden from His sight, but all things are naked and open to the eyes of Him to whom we must give account.
Diligence requires us to be awake and to take action by putting on Christ, aware of the devices of the enemy and the possibility of our slackness from living right.

This is where conviction comes into effect, when we do drift and when we have not matured in some areas, this is ongoing, the search light of the Holy Spirit will highlight the darkness in our soul, testing our motivations and the purity of our faith. Even our other brother will experience the soul searching light, as he strays from the compassion of Christ, looking down on his wayward brother.
Hebrews 10:35, 36
35 Therefore do not cast away your confidence, which has great reward.
36 For you have need of endurance, so that after you have done the will of God, you may receive the promise:
Any purification process needs to go through to completion, remain in His care and trust Him for the outcome.
Hebrews 10:37-39
37 "For yet a little while,
And He who is coming will come and will not tarry.
38 Now the just shall live by faith;
But if anyone draws back,
My soul has no pleasure in him."

39 But we are not of those who draw back to perdition, but of those who believe to the saving of the soul.
Don't run away from the process of faith, keep believing and remain in Him, no matter what it looks like on the surface where the impurities rise due to the heat, the Father knows the end product and sees the completion of our faith.

Hebrews 4:14-16
14 Seeing then that we have a great High Priest who has passed through the heavens, Jesus the Son of God, let us hold fast our confession.
15 For we do not have a High Priest who cannot sympathize with our weaknesses, but was in all points tempted as we are, yet without sin.
16 Let us therefore come boldly to the throne of grace, that we may obtain mercy and find grace to help in time of need.

Grace is about getting help when our weaknesses are exposed and brought to the light by His word that lays bear our frailties, in the light of His perfect character we will come undone, to the point that His Word penetrates and can judge the intents and heart motivations.
We need help in these times to bring us through our challenges and temptations to conform us to His image of the overcomer, imprinted in our DNA from above.

Grace is all about His One New Man becoming a reality in our lives, rising above the patterns of our old ways.

His word is spirit and life.

His word for you is who you really are in Him and there is life in His image of the plan, to activate all He has planned for you in the hope of your future. Now a light is shining in a dark place that replaces the old pattern of life with the New Creation and the Holy Spirit will raise you up into the plan.
When the spotlight is on us and darkness seems to rule, when we can't see any hope of a future at times, as the road seems just too long and hard.
Hang in There!
When we have blown it big time and there just doesn't seem to be a way out of our messed up stuff anymore.
This is the time to receive His help. Go to the Throne of Grace in that time of no way out and receive His help from above.

Don't give up!

There is a place we can go for mercy, as we all fall short and whether we stray a long way off, or we are near and have wrong attitudes, we can come to Jesus and freely receive a fresh start, yesterday has gone and the failures of our past won't stop our future, when we come to Him for grace.

Which is His ability to live in the **ONE NEW MAN** that He has made by His sacrifice and payment on our behalf, He would find no pleasure if we don't agree with who He says we have become with the eyes of faith.

Under grace and no longer under the law.
What does it mean?
Well let me say it doesn't mean if we are doing the law that we are in trouble.
If you obey the commandments of God there is a blessing as in Deuteronomy 28 and Psalm 119 show the benefits of obedience and it is healthy to remain within the laws and commandments of God.

What was the other brother doing that placed him near but without compassion and wrong attitudes?
Was he busy and full of activities that were within the law and in the nearness of doing the right thing by God? He was convinced that he was OK, as he was on the program.
Sometimes we can become so program and doing the plan focused, that we lose sight of who we are serving and our connection to the Father of our spirits.

It is possible to once again, to be *me* focused on *my* efforts and achievements and forgetting the source of our expression and who we really are. There is the grace factor, free gift, and unearned favour.

We are children of God, co heirs with Jesus and friends of the Holy Spirit.
This is a love partnership and connection and that is our heart motivation.

Working and doing is a good thing, but it is the function and the outward expression of something inwardly more precious and heart felt. We are working with Him as well as for Him, in our journey of discovery of the real me and the me I am meant to be. It is me, but it is all about Him.

If you are the director and founder of a company of your own creation and a very ambitious employee worked hard and one day decided, *"I am making this company work and I no longer need the director, I am taking over, as I work best and the director is now redundant as he has done what is required by launching me in the company."*

There would be a problem.

The Obedience of Christ

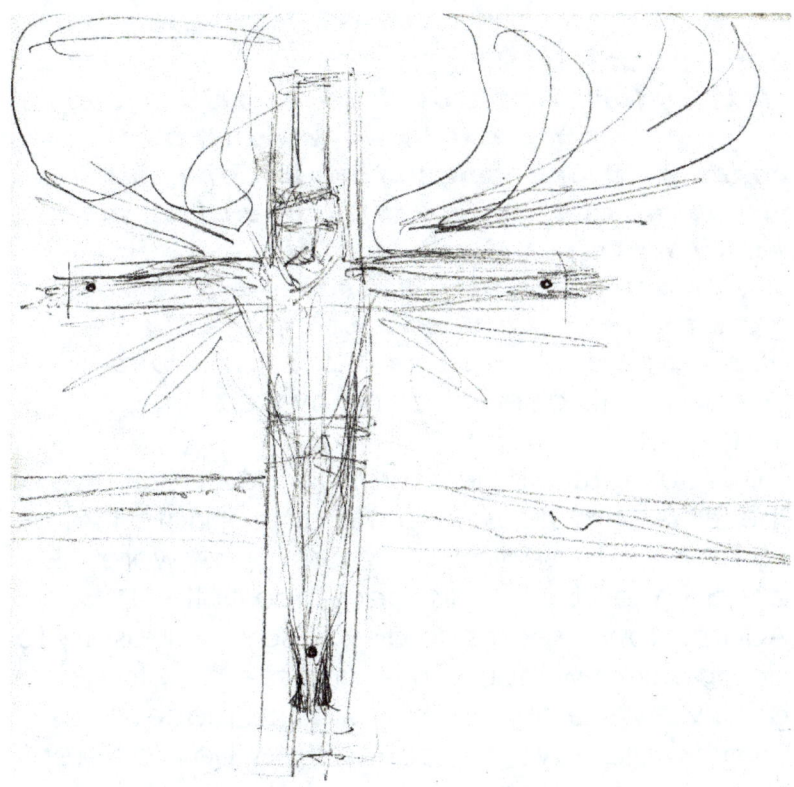

Copyright © March 2025

There was a First Adam and then there came a Second Adam.
Does our obedience differ?
Don't try to be another Christ!!!
Romans 5:14
14 Nevertheless death reigned from Adam to Moses, even over those who had not sinned according to the likeness of the transgression of Adam, who is a type of Him who was to come.

So there are those that sinned alright, but not in the likeness or same way that Adam did.

Romans 5:18, 19
18 ***Therefore, as through one man's offense judgment came to all men, resulting in condemnation, even so through one Man's righteous act the free gift came to all men, resulting in justification of life.***
19 ***For as by one man's disobedience many were made sinners, so also by one Man's obedience many will be made righteous.***
By one man's obedience many were <u>made</u> righteous!!!
This is our righteousness through the obedience of the 2nd Adam Jesus, what He appropriated for us, by His act of obedience. Whereas, we were all condemned by the disobedience of the 1st Adam. Now it seems unfair you say, well just try to be obedient without Christ and see how far you go, if we were put in the 1st Adams place, guess what would have happened? Maybe a different playing out, but the result would be there, in a way we all do go through the same thing, slightly innocent when we were a child, but following up with the same disposition of the fallen man Adam.
What is our obedience?

Romans 5:17
17 ***For if by the one man's offense death reigned through the one, much more those who receive abundance of grace and of the gift of righteousness will reign in life through the One, Jesus Christ.***

Those who <u>receive</u> is the key word and is our obedience, it is an entering into and the act of faith, as we receive His benefits when He rose from the dead, the death of our disobedience in the 1st Adam to be made righteous in the obedience in the 2nd Adam. As children of God let's receive what the Father has provided to us and live in the faith through the Son of God.

Now we are all in a process of change and along the way there are temptations that will test our weaknesses and bring to our attention what is lacking in our faith, as it is refined to purity like gold.
That is why we need grace to obey.
1 John 5:3
3 For this is the love of God, that we keep His commandments.
And His commandments are not burdensome.

John 14:15
15 "If you love Me, keep My commandments.
Psalm 119:33-35
33 Teach me, O Lord, the way of Your statutes,
And I shall keep it to the end.
34 Give me understanding, and I shall keep Your law;
Indeed, I shall observe it with my whole heart.
35 Make me walk in the path of Your commandments,
For I delight in it.

God sees the heart of man and that he or she is willing to humble themselves to receive from Him as our God and Saviour.
Man looks at the outside and sees the performance of he or she and makes judgements and acceptance based on this perception.

Psalm 40:6-8
6 Sacrifice and offering You did not desire;
My ears You have opened.
Burnt offering and sin offering You did not require.
7 Then I said, "Behold, I come;
In the scroll of the book it is written of me.
8 I delight to do Your will, O my God,
And Your law is within my heart."

Jesus came to do The will of the Father, His will done on earth and in it achieved a new genealogy and bloodline for his body, the church to receive new life to be the new man who says like King David, *"I delight to do your will, O my God"* and notice where does this new found gift or grace come from? "Your law is written in my heart". This is newness of life and not the oldness of the external knowledge of the law.

2 Timothy 1:7
7 For God has not given us a spirit of fear, but of power and of love and of a sound mind.
Which leads into another significant number three, which is the three temptations of Jesus.

The devils temptation, strategies are still the same old techniques that he uses on mankind, luring us by cunning deceit, to become independent from the Father and live like we are a god, ruling our own destiny by self promoted greatness.

The devil fell in pride and arrogance and became void of the light of love, entering into a wicked darkness, in a lawless independence of selfish desires, which sent paradise on earth into a state of a fallen, chaotic world in madness and evil intentions, he deceives us to believe that thinking that we know better than God is a knowledge to be desired.

He fell from being the highest ranking and beautifully adorned creation of the angels, with much talents and glory to being a grotesque, crooked winged creature, in a hideous darkness, surrounded by flies – not to be desired.

The three temptations that Satan devised for Jesus in His time of testing:-
1. Command the bread – control your own supply without asking God in prayer and use any source of power to get what you want.
2. Throw yourself down – you decide your own fate, commanding God to protect you, whatever you do.
3. Fall down and worship Satan– worship the principle of self rule and lust to gain anything in this world – *do what thou will.*

The Devil came to Jesus, foolishly hoping to make Him become like Satan became after his fall – separated from the wisdom of God and disconnected in his life choices.

The Devil was hoping to tempt the 2nd Adam to fall away from the Kingdom of God and rule of the Father, like he succeeded in doing with the 1st Adam.
However, Jesus did not yield to the Devil and resisted him and in His victory, we can now gain our victory to overcome the works of the devil in this life.
Jesus rightly answered in the first temptation *"man does not live by bread alone but by every word that proceeds from the Father"*.

This shows his dependence on the Father and as a son, his obedience to follow the leading of the Father and not by his own appetites.
It is interesting that He was asked to command bread into existence from stones. We are all like stones and that could mean that we can create our own word of authority from within ourselves, to feed us with a control to be a god of our own world that we create at will. Kind of dark energised stones.

The reality is that we are not all knowing and not developed to make all of the right choices without waiting on a spoken word from the Father, a *Rhema* is instruction to us to lead us the right way.

We can seek Him in the relationship as His sons and daughters desiring to know what is best, He speaks to us in many ways, as we come to know Him better on our journey and maturity into all truth.

Psalm 119:105
105 *Your word is a lamp to my feet.*
And a light unto my path.

The whole aim of the devil when he tempts someone, is to take them from their connection and dependence on the Father to be disconnected and autonomous, having a rule of their own, in a matrix system that is constructed separate from Gods Kingdom.

He will challenge your sonship or daughter relationship to entice us by offering what he proposes is a better way and dressed up as freedom, which is in reality rebellion from the Lordship of God. We will become like the Devil is - orphaned from the family of God, no longer under the protection of the Fathers house, we will be outcast and separated by an independent, self rule, following the ways of our own soul. There are basically two camps and no inbetweens; either you are in the Kingdom of God and serve under His rule and remain under His care and protection.

Or you are separated by a choice of self rule, which places you under serving the devil.

As this is the worship the devil wants, that you come into agreement with his ways, which is rebellion and a lawlessness, turning away from God.

Now when we are deceived into this path, it removes us from the protection and wholeness that Gods ways provide and leads us into a path of destruction, this consequence the devil will cunningly not mention.

When we realize what the result of our choices brings like Adam and Eve – we might hear the devil saying in mocking tones, *"Oh dear oh dear, did I not mention that? Well that's the price of freedom, so just take it on the chin and suck it up! You might as well hang out in my place, it's hot and forever burning, but you better get used to it!"*

Someone called Jesus good once and He replied only the Father is good! – but Jesus was sinless??? – Yes! He was! He said *"it is the Father who lives in Me that does the works"*. Jesus as a man was still entirely dependant on the Father for His substance to be righteous and to be a Son, He had to learn obedience to draw from the genes, if you like or the DNA of the living Father and not break away, into an independent spirit that no longer needs God as His source.
The lure of sin comes from the *Tree of Knowledge of Good and Evil*.

Has the alluring appearance of:-
1. *Good to eat.*
2. *Good to look upon.*
3. *Good for knowledge.*

You can be like a god!

Is the *Tree of Knowledge of Good and Evil* bad or is it that we just can't handle that freedom of choice, without connecting to the ONE who could - Jesus?

The 3rd eye is talked about a lot for the ones seeking enlightenment and who want to develop the imagination.
God created the imagination and it is a gateway into the spirit world and the visual arena for creativity and shouldn't be despised.
However, there is such a thing as the imagination being darkened.

Ephesians 4:18
18 *having their understanding darkened, being alienated from the life of God, because of the ignorance that is in them, because of the blindness of their heart;*

The word is understanding, but can be translated to imagination, as the part of your mind that is enlightened and can see abstract or surreal things.

So what happened when Adam and Eve ate the forbidden fruit? Their eyes were opened to another way of seeing things.

It wasn't that they didn't have an imagination or that they couldn't see into the spirit world, as they were freely able to see into the hidden realm and the natural world readily without fear or restraint.

So what happened?

I have a feeling that their eyes of the imagination became darkened and this opened up an ability to think and imagine evil intent and see things outside of Gods healthy boundaries into dark thoughts, so they were ashamed as they were naked. Loss of innocence came to them similar to when a child grows to that certain age and their thinking is darkened, which results in what a decline of the imagination. Of cause they aren't all bad, they still have good thoughts as well, but the capacity and the inclination is now there, to go down a wrong track of twisted and crooked perceptions.

It appears that as we progress down the dark track, that it dulls the senses in the imagination realm and our eyes become dark, by a gross darkness that shrouds our thinking in the state some would imagine to be free, on the contrary it actually bounds us into the decaying universe.

What about new technology like Google Glasses? Well a whole new way of seeing things isn't it? Expand our vision and minds. Technology in itself isn't evil, but the dark imaginations combined will utilize and create the monster.

Another step towards our future in the brave new world and collective seeing and thinking within the beast. The gruesome, great collective database of knowledge.

Thank God that He created one new man in Jesus.

There seems to be two main tendencies of human nature under the fall, with variations and degrees and blendings of the two, as all are unique and subject to change. Either you will go astray and squander the gift and inheritance in reckless living – do as you will and your own will be done.

Or you will be self righteous and expect a reward, but never feel worthy to receive it until you achieve an ultimate level of service, in your spiritual pursuit, seemingly close to the ways of God and righteous living and then, you will despise someone accepted back in who doesn't deserve it, by not living a disciplined life like you have.

Gods plan is that both need to enter into the one new man in Christ, to bring them into their inheritance and acceptance from the Father by way of the blood of Jesus; which qualifies them to be sons and daughters and receive the blessings of God and the ability to walk in His ways.

We live in hope that the Son of God came to destroy the works of the devil, which disabled us into a default position of missing the mark and unable to live right, but now by faith; we may enter into a new man created in His image of which a seed was placed in our being, with the potential to grow into the completed work of Christ in us, the blessed hope of Glory.
He who does the will of God enters into the new man by faith and abides in this truth and ability to be the brand new person, who is created by God in newness of the life that He designed for us to be in by Christ Jesus.

It is like Jesus telling us to come and walk on the water, it is a faith step and walk in a new unlimited man, not filled with fear and inability to achieve the impossible, but receives the new ability to walk above the storms and contrary waves of what is familiar and what nature throws at us. In our natural state, which is the default from the first Adam, who fell into a life separated and independent from God, we are subject to the storms of life and are tossed about by the waves, as we are unable to rise above what is overwhelming and this will send us either a long way off from God, or to striving against the pressures to live right and hoping one day we will reach some kind of level of perfection, to gain approval and our inheritance from God for our good works. That is why this brother or the other brother would despise the one who drifts away and is reckless as his way is so far off, so different to he, who wants to live in the right way.

In the new man we can enjoy the gift of righteousness and the new ability to live right based on love and acceptance from the Father as sons in His Kingdom, therefore, we can now enter into and partake of the blessings, freely given to the liberated sons and daughters of God.

Enter into the Purification Process by faith into who He says you have become in Him.
Receive what He has provided for you by faith, as He is pure you are pure also.
Draw from the Resurrection Life that raised Him from the dead to also raise you up above the constraints and the powers that keep you in bondage to sin.
Sin shall not have dominion over you.

You are a co-heir with Christ.
Identify with His death and Resurrection and enter into this process by the acceptance of what He has freely provided – this is the transaction that credits you with Righteousness and the ability to enter into the process.
See yourself as He sees you in newness of life, no longer captive to the old that is in corruption.
In Him we are Holy as He is Holy.

As He is so are we in the world.
We are His workmanship created in Christ Jesus for good works.
Receive the good works that are prepared for you to enter into.

What is the process like?

Ever felt like your inner chatter is not always on your side? Self talk can be a good coach or a bad coach depending on what frame of mind you are in.

On your positive bio-rhythm on the upside your mood is upbeat, ready to take on the world, but when that momentum flips to the negative for all sorts of reasons, we take on another persona, who wants to tell us how badly we missed it and we are never going to rise again.

Galatians 5:16-18
16 I say then: Walk in the Spirit, and you shall not fulfill the lust of the flesh.
17 For the flesh lusts against the Spirit, and the Spirit against the flesh; and these are contrary to one another, so that you do not do the things that you wish.
18 But if you are led by the Spirit, you are not under the law.

It is like a cat fight at times as your fleshly, old man nature does not want to let go of its dominance in your life. Have you seen two cats fighting?
They go hard at it and there's a lot of hissing, scratching, biting and they spin around looking for a vicious strike to take out the opposition.

You will need to feed your white cat on the Word of God, stay in prayer and in an atmosphere of worship, remain in good company, where the white cat can be encouraged to be strong, pray in the spirit to sharpen the claws in revelation truth, to defeat the dark cat who isn't going to back down without a good rumble tumble!!!
Remember the old Indians tale, whichever you feed the most wins!

There are many strategies to overcome and in each person's individual case, their black cat will have a different personality and its own unique resistance.
So, if you find yourself getting knocked about and the black cat does have some ongoing dominance, don't expect defeat, trust God and His process to bring you through, He has begun a good work in you and plans to bring it to completion,
so, as long as we allow Him to be Lord of our lives, He will direct your paths to victory no matter what you face.

Titus 2:11-14
11 For the grace of God that brings salvation has appeared to all men,
12 teaching us that, denying ungodliness and worldly lusts, we should live soberly, righteously, and godly in the present age,
13 looking for the blessed hope and glorious appearing of our great God and Savior Jesus Christ,

14 *who gave Himself for us, that He might redeem us from every lawless deed and purify for Himself His own special people, zealous for good works.*

We have received a grace gift to teach us and show us the way to live righteously, if we lack the know how and the desire to deny our worldly lusts, we can draw upon a grace from God as believers, to rise above the low living as we have a hope that Jesus came to purify our deeds and make us one with Him, we are a special people through His gift, motivated towards good works.

Titus 3:4-7
4 *But when the kindness and the love of God our Savior toward man appeared,*
5 *not by works of righteousness which we have done, but according to His mercy He saved us, through the washing of regeneration and renewing of the Holy Spirit,*
6 *whom He poured out on us abundantly through Jesus Christ our Savior,*
7 *that having been justified by His grace we should become heirs according to the hope of eternal life.*

Thank God for His kindness and we are reminded that our salvation is by grace and not based upon our own righteousness, or self righteousness, but what Jesus came to provide for us in the new life as the one new person in Him.

The regenerating work of the Holy Spirit has transformed us into His image and likeness and we become heirs, as His brothers and sisters in the family of God with our Father in Heaven, who we are forever grateful for accepting us, based on what Jesus has done.

Receive His love as He runs towards you and embraces you as you return to Him and receive His love and the regeneration from your old life, as either a lost son who went their own direction in life and ended up in the pig pen, or the near son who has misunderstood the love of the Father and hasn't entered into all of the benefits of an heir with joy and gladness, who was comparing his performance to another, but now is renewed and just enjoying the presence and love of the Father.
Now for a three level development process:-
Romans 12:1, 2
1 beseech you therefore, brethren, by the mercies of God, that you present your bodies a living sacrifice, holy, acceptable to God, which is your reasonable service.
2 And do not be conformed to this world, but be transformed by the renewing of your mind, that you may prove what is that good and acceptable and perfect will of God.
It is reasonable, to offer ourselves considering what He is offering us and calling us to be in exchange in this world, through the ability of Christ.

There are three levels of entering into His will beginning with the good, then acceptable and then the perfect level *(30, 60, 100)* and this is in accordance with our agreement with the image that He has placed inside us.

Christ in us and the renewal of our minds, enables us to see ourselves as He sees us and declares us to be and we will then accordingly, find His will in ever increasing levels. The pattern of this world that held us in bondage and hindered our service to God, will increasingly have less influence, reaching a mature level of no hold on us, in the perfect will of God. When developing our strength in training levels, we gradually increase our ability to reach our best potential.

The patterns of this world have shaped us into the potential of man without God and shape us through inherited weakness and character traits and the influence, from the environment of worldly, humanistic thinking, which is the effects of philosophy and the mindset of our times, this will shape our potential away from the higher ways and mind of God.

The following versus in Romans 12 speak about the grace gifts that each one has been given. We are also provided with a measure of faith, which is our motivation to achieve our calling of God, despite the hindrances experienced and our many weaknesses and failures to perform.

Our focus is to see ourselves through His eyes, made whole and empowered by the Holy Spirit. Activated by the destiny and motivation of God motivates us into the new creation of our true identity and potential.

We are now one with our brother from above who is Lord and above all, we are made new from the old striving and harsh man of the other brother and the destructive, wanderings of his prodigal brother.

You are a new creation, Oh Brother, Oh Sister.

Diversity meets the Other

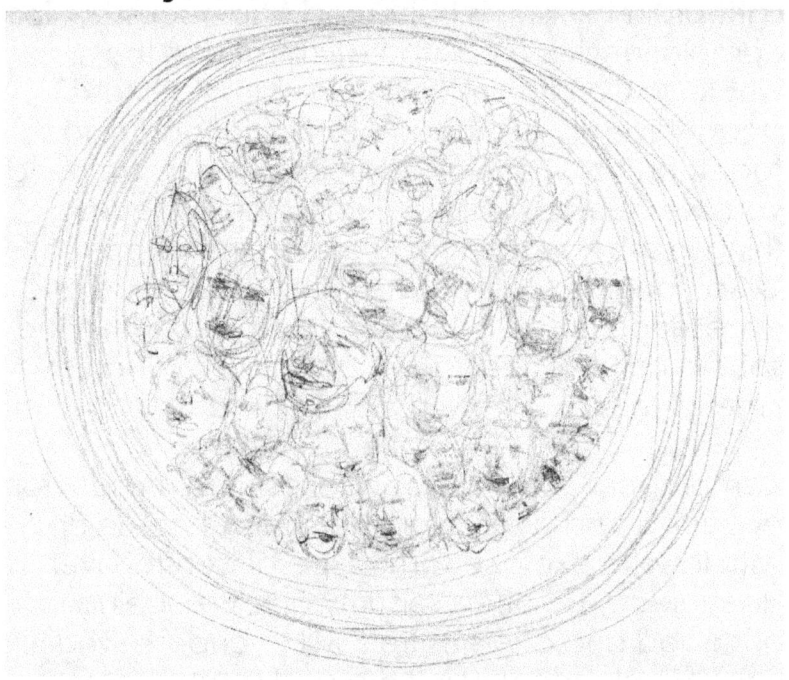

Let us bring two opposites together to form divine order.

Left and Right Brain thinking, yes surprise, we need both to have both sides of the story.
An overall perspective.

The creative and the practical go together.
Let me now bring Pauls teaching on what – yes that's right, diversity. Paul mentions diversity and the need for it, do you mean this concept was taught 2 thousand years ago? Correct!!! Nothing new under the sun.

Diversity, yes Paul taught diversity both left and right brain thinking is honoured and necessary for completion, it is a collaboration to form the whole. In Corinthians and Ephesians Paul talks about diversity of gifts and operations coming together, not a one sided point of view. We need you, we need everybody doing their unique thing in other words, if you are on the fringe that's OK as long as you operate within the image and excellence how God made you to be, within the sphere of influence you would have for such a time as this.

Remember, God has boundaries for a reason, for our good and protection, He doesn't come up with laws to exercise some type of control over His subjects, He offers security and well-being for our good and offers us free will to choose what is right. He placed you in time and space before time began to be and do. Your uniqueness adds to the diversity of gifts and talents and individual expression. You were uniquely crafted as an individual and part of the multi-faceted splendour of God in His creation, no one else can do life like you do. Diversity – God created it and He saw that it is good.

Let me propose a new concept for all the Greek Minded logical thinkers out there, lets reason this out, lets be objective – I propose Diversity in HIM is Godly Order and will prosper, Diversity contrived by Men's Traditions, Agendas' and Philosophies are harmful by tainted ideologies.

Which do you prefer a twisted and limited mind view or Gods infinite wisdom guiding the ship? So, bring it on, Diversity in HIM under the Lordship of Jesus and we will be smooth sailing. I can't wait for the positive feedback from this comment.
AS we know from true history untainted by a false history narrative, that all Languages and Cultures, Diverse Peoples, originated at the Tower of Babel. This all occurred after Nimrod united people under a Globalist Agenda Reign that was ahead of its time. However, this reign was headed for total corruption and rampant evil in control of all under its totalitarian rule. That information will go down really well, that utopia was a horror show and God had to stop the untied vision under the spell of the evil agenda hive mind by splitting the peoples into the basis of 70 nations for all people groups that exist today. Otherwise, if they were permitted to continue opening up the portal to hell and allowing pure evil from the underworld into our realm it would have resulted in a monster show global village nightmare.

Fortunately, the world was spared from this annihilation by God creating languages, confusing their plans and also bringing further diversity of people and they were no longer united by these evil intentions. What this means for us today is that all people groups, nations, are derived from the 3 sons of Noah, so we are all related by traceable DNA, even if we are black, brown, red, yellow and white.

But in Christ we are ONE yet diverse, that's called unity and working together for the common good, all looking after everyone else, true equality, yep Paul taught on that two thousand years ago. We don't mean a defiled equality based on secular ideologies.

Colossians 3:11
11 where there is neither Greek nor Jew, circumcised nor uncircumcised, barbarian, Scythian, slave nor free, but Christ is all and in all.

Conclusion

Take His hand and allow Him to guide you through the process of change into the one new man in Christ Jesus, as you become the unique, God particle person that He created you to be and this is found in Jesus, as He came to give us the life we are destined to have.
He took our distorted values and gave us His life and virtues.

Virtue (Meanings explained from Greek lexicon):-
Any excellence of a person body or mind, an eminent endowment, property or quality.
His excellencies, perfections that shine forth in our gratuitous callings and in the whole work of our salvation.

2 Peter 1:2-4
2 Grace and peace be multiplied to you in the knowledge of God and of Jesus our Lord,

3 as His divine power has given to us all things that pertain to life and godliness, through the knowledge of Him who called us by glory and virtue,
4 by which have been given to us exceedingly great and precious promises, that through these you may be partakers of the divine nature, having escaped the corruption that is in the world through lust.

Escape the corruption of this world ruled by lust. How, can it possibly happen?

Whoever you are, far away like the lost prodigal, or near like the other brother.
ENTER into the promise of virtue by faith – receive His divine power and be a partaker of the divine nature of the One New Man.
Faith replaces our attempts to be righteous.
Faith will produce action and the outcome of the good works that we were created in Christ Jesus to walk in.

Paul the Apostle was a profoundly influential Apostle in terms of impacting the world with the Good News of Jesus Christ and contributing much of the revelations in the New Testament Bible. He opened up *"the just shall live by faith"* teaching and *"by grace we are saved and this is not from ourselves, by our own works of the law."* He showed that Jewish traditions tried to obtain a righteousness by the law and did not find the righteousness by faith that Abraham the father of faith found.

Abraham having a body that was aged and good as dead believed God to do what He said He would perform, a miracle in his earthly body of death, creating new life and the promised child, born by the power of God.
When Paul first established a Gentile church, the Jewish believers sneaked into his meetings hoping to spy on the new found freedom of living the Gospel of faith in Jesus and the new found freedom from the constraints of trying to live by the law apart from God.
There is an obedience based on who we are, which is not based on what we have done.

Paul mentions that we are not to judge our brother, where they are at in their faith walk. The brother who keeps customs and rituals is not to judge the one who doesn't keep those rituals and practices, the one who has freedom not to keep the practices, also needs to respect where the other brother is at and why he is dependent on those practices, helping him to find his faith.

There is also jealousy evident by those that see their brothers in liberty and the gifts of God flowing through them, the favour of God is upon them, provoking the religious brother to jealousy when he sees miracles and testimonies in abundance on his brothers.

However, Paul did not start out preaching with a demonstration of the Sprit and power in the liberty, as an accepted son of God.

He began his purpose in his own wisdom and abilities, in his own understanding of religion and the traditions of men. Paul was a man of intense religious practices and a respected leader of the Pharisees, the governing Jewish Sect of the day.

Paul was high and mighty in the ranks of the Pharisees and could not tolerate the new believers in Jesus Christ, persecuting them, hunting them down and killing them in the name of religious law, believing that he was God's policeman on earth.

Paul who was known as Saul got knocked off his horse spectacularly, by a brilliant white light from Heaven above, in the person of Jesus who is the Son of God.

Paul was on a supposed mission from God to rid the earth of believers from the early Christian church, until the light blinded him and the truth about Jesus stopped him in his tracks.

Later, after he saw the light and repented, scales came off his eyes, he got his name changed by God and in the new identity as God really saw him, he could now truly see as a changed man. Paul was an example of the ultimate other brother, resenting his brothers who had a different faith and a freedom that enraged him to commit murder in the name of religion.

We can trace the trouble and differences, all of the way back to the very first brothers Cain and Abel, "brother you are so different and a pain and I don't like you". Cain killed Abel in a fit of rage.

Conflict still exists today in relationships, even in our technologically advancing world, a similar instance is illustrated by the story of the Prodigal Son and his resentful brother.

God sent His only Son into the world of strife, to save us and bring us all back into His family of love. God is a good Father and wants His children to receive freely His good gifts, even when we didn't earn it.

How can we best illustrate brothers in conflict and what is the solution?

Why is it a common theme that extends into nations versus nations?

Take the example of Jacob whose name means deceiver with his twin brother Esau, their descendants are now in the hot spot known as the Middle East.

The wounds go deep into the DNA, setting up future actions and reactions, which are expressed into rage and wars and rumours of wars.

In Jacobs and Esau's case there were the issues of parental bias, imbalances and favorites in upbringing which influenced the twin brothers Jacob and Esau. We have the classic jealousy scenarios, great plots for movies, differences, cheating, deception and bitterness was evident in this relationship of dramas.

The shocking thing is that these brothers are the offspring of the promised child Isaac.
Jacob who inherited the blessings by deception later became Israel after wrestling with God, indeed he was an interesting and colourful person.

These brothers are the epitome of family disputes followed by generational divisions, conflict and wars that exist today, which we can read about on the news.

The Middle East with Arab nations all surrounding Israel where Jacobs trouble erupts almost daily, the descendants of these brothers take the feud into modern military reactions with rocket firing and modern warfare weaponry battles. Then all we need to do is step back to the prior generation of contention and strife with Jacobs father Isaac, who was the promised child of Abraham,
but Abraham produced Ishmael and these grew up amongst controversy, conflict and jealousy. What a history to get things rolling, all of these emotions are deeply embedded into the bloodlines of these brothers in conflict. The Middle East and the conflicts that occur there remain evident in this troubled world with wars, terrorism, rockets continually fired into the other brothers camp and fired back again in revenge, so it carries on. Just like those feuds of families that go back into history, never forgotten, a festering sore point and a reason to continue in revenge, tit for tat.

Actions produce a ripple effect. What sins the parents commit will trickle down into the following generations, iniquity embeds like a virus into the psyche of the following generations DNA programmed responses.

Exodus 34:6-7 New King James Version (NKJV)
6 And the Lord passed before him and proclaimed, "The Lord, the Lord God, merciful and gracious, longsuffering, and abounding in goodness and truth,
7 keeping mercy for thousands, forgiving iniquity and transgression and sin, by no means clearing the guilty, visiting the iniquity of the fathers upon the children and the children's children to the third and the fourth generation."

Here is the duality, there is mercy and compassion as well as justice and consequences. So, compassion and mercy is the response to justice and consequences, but it is a legal transaction, it must be enacted and chosen and requires an act to redeem something that is under the law.
So a negative consequence can only be corrected by a powerful overwhelming positive action.
Romans 5:18-21
18 Therefore, as through one man's offense judgment came to all men, resulting in condemnation, even so through one Man's righteous act the free gift came to all men, resulting in justification of life.

***19** For as by one man's disobedience many were made sinners, so also by one Man's obedience many will be made righteous.*
***20** Moreover the law entered that the offense might abound. But where sin abounded, grace abounded much more,*
***21** so that as sin reigned in death, even so grace might reign through righteousness to eternal life through Jesus Christ our Lord.*

Adams sin produced death and judgment and by generational inheritance we all became sinners, as we all fall short somewhere and choose to sin.
Jesus action created a new life which has over written our DNA by His blood, purifying us into a new creation.
Grace is abounding to all who receive it by faith, renouncing their old ways and accepting the new path ways of the gift of righteousness.
We need grace in abundance to counteract the following:
Action of Cain killing Abel = consequence, murder hatred.
Actions of our faith champions Abraham Sarah, they were still human,
Actions of Isaac and Ishmael,
Actions of Jacob and Esau,
= consequence, conflicts between brothers and then consequently nations, different races.
Parents actions repeated patterns of behaviour in children, = consequence, Jacob lying and cheating using deception.

How can this be reversed?
God knew His Son is the only way the actions of creating iniquitous patterns of behaviour can be reversed, performed by the redemptive action of Jesus.
It is in the blood, you've heard of bad blood, well how can this be corrected?
Only by good blood. Jesus was the only righteous person to exist and He was the only one qualified to deal with generations of bad blood. His righteous blood cleanses our very DNA from all of the bad blood memories and echoes of our past generations that have stained us and set us up for conflict and strife against our prodigal brothers and other brothers in this world.
When you have a negative force you need a positive force to take it away or cancel its effects.

Nothing but the blood of Jesus can take it away.
God has a solution to our pollution.
Faith is the action key and Grace pays the price and allows a legal change to take place.
The cancellation of curses and ordinances written against us is a reality.

Paul wrote about two powerful prayers of transformation in the Book of Ephesians.
He prayed that the eyes of our imagination would be opened to see the possibilities that God sees in this world, for you and me and those that we interact with.

We have an exceedingly great, resurrection power given to us by Christ to accomplish what God sees, for our future impact in this world.

Our imagination is reignited by the power of love, we soar with enhanced insight into higher dimensions and our youth is renewed like the eagles, beyond the natural into the realms of faith where all things are possible.

His love passes what we have experienced in the natural, transforming our behaviour, into a higher perspective, beyond what we would normally imagine.

Christ in us will bring more than we can imagine or are capable of asking into our reality. When we have the eyes of faith, we will come into agreement with the greater works and seeing the answer like God sees the answer.

I feel the message in this book is relevant for the troubled times that we are in today and the times we will face in the future, as we aim to build a better world.

In the book of 1 Corinthians Chapter 12, the Apostle Paul mentions diversity of gifts and diversity in operations. These gifts and functions are present in the whole Body of Christ and originate from a diverse group of people from all races, colour, backgrounds, social status and you name it, left brain, right brain, we are all different and are inter dependent on one another.

We are all uniquely made and created like the colours of a rainbow, displaying a diverse array of people groups. (Written in 2013, rainbow has different meanings currently, however the rainbow is God's, so it is beautiful. We just need to remain within Gods boundaries how He created it. Muddy colours wont work) We are all connected by a DNA thread in generational lines, originating in the Genesis created by One God. We are made in His image, so there is an interconnected relationship and characteristics shared between all.

Actually the philosophy of a big Global Village of diverse races and people groups is not new, it is all there laid out in the plan of God who is building His structure, a holy temple filled with multi cultural, multi faceted people coming together in unity based on the love of God, being of one mind and one spirit.
We are all part of a coloured spectrum of variety, mingled together with different personalities and how we view the world. Why so different, because God is infinitely diverse and unfathomable, He created each one different as reflecting an aspect of Himself, we are unique and a separate entity having our own will and mind to make decisions and create in our time and place.

Together we are meant to make up a habitation where God lives in His Temple, which is His Kingdom within us, His Spirit fills our beings creating us from dark masses into living stones.

It is not a question of whose side you are on. Conservative or Liberal. Black or White, Right or Left. God isn't about taking sides with this party or another. Either side of the fence, the left or right can set themselves up as judge and jury, hanging all who don't agree with their opinions on a high and mighty horse, only to be knocked off by the brightness of the glory light of God's righteousness and justice, speaking the truth in love.

Be careful then not to reject everybody that comes from a particular group, race, party, country, because the narrative painted doesn't fit your own philosophies.

There is good and bad in all groups. The Commander in charge, Jesus has come from above, not to take sides, but to unite all and bring out the best from all our differences, refine by fire all that doesn't have the characteristics of love due to prejudices, preconceived notions and wrong thinking about others and how we view the world.

Perfect love erases all fear, fight and fright becomes a renewed mind of peace and goodwill towards all people everywhere. It isn't all about who is right and who is wrong; it is about His Kingdom coming and the brightness of His light expelling the darkness.

*Yes, Jesus has a standard, it is the perfect law where there is no shadows, mixtures of good and evil, no duality it is complete in purity.
Which means we are being conformed into His image, we are created new, we are in the process of being perfected and learning to operate within the perfect laws of love.*

We either fall off our wayward horse like the Prodigal son, or we are knocked off our religious horse like Paul who was like the other brother.

*Jesus is the truth, which means He is not embracing anything that is opposed to the truth, He has come to reveal the truth, expel all Darkness by His Light.
Jesus came to destroy all of the works of the enemy, therefore, all of the false doctrines of man, false religions, pride and self righteousness are rejected offerings and will be displaced by the purity of God's Glory. His Kingdom come on earth as it is in Heaven. His Plans are Higher than our Plans, so give it up!
It is the compassion of God that leads us to change our mind and direction in life, we change how we view others into the perspective from above. We are now renewed in the likeness of the Man from Heaven and no longer reflect the self governing man from the earth.
Collaboration means that we take the strengths from different talents and work together for a cohesive plan, combining strengths and supporting weaknesses, being a more complete team effort to reach a goal.*

From Acts 2 in the Bible is found a collaborative effort.

The Early Believers in Jesus Christ established a community where all had in common and they shared resources and the surplus was distributed fairly and all was done in one accord. Why? They were one with God in spirit and truth, so they had as their heart motivation, the love of God.

In summary they saw others through the eyes of the Father who loves His children and He has their best interests for them.

Everyone has a destiny and a purpose, but they firstly need to be connected in a relationship with Father God, who can position each one and allow each ones thinking to be redirected to be a positive contributor in this world for the common good.

The One New Man is created in Christ Jesus, as only God's love and Mind can bring together such diversity and cultural differences into one body of believers, who are submitted to Him as the Head and submitted to one another in respect of each gift that all offer, as nourishment to the whole.

Paul once was the epitome of a self righteous judgmental brother, who was dramatically changed into a new creation and he was united with his brothers in the one new man, in Jesus Christ.

Although he was Jewish, he became a mighty Apostle that brought the Gospel and deliverance to the Gentiles. Jews and Gentiles are now united in faith, in the one new man, those who are far off are one with those who are near to God.

It is a beautiful world.
So let's work together in the spirit of the one new man and together, create a better place for all.

This is God's dream world of Utopia, Heaven on Earth.

"Older Brother the Other"

By Peter Koren
ISBN: 978-1-0670653-4-8
PaperBack

Published by GLOWING LIGHT LTD
Auckland New Zealand
Copyright © 2025

Original Copyright © April 2014 from earlier versions using titles,
The Other Brother and Brother! You didn't Earn it!

www.beinginthelight.com

Cover Art by Peter Koren.

Interior Illustrations Art Work by Peter Koren.

Copyright © 2021

Images used for cover design with permission
Public Domain CC0 Image
https://www.pxfuel.com/en/free-photo-ojyrx
man, young, city, hoodie, arms crossed, thunderstorm, electric, dark, night, male
Death Valley National Park, United States. Original public domain image from Wikimedia Commons
Rock formations line the horizon of Oljato-Monument Valley. Original public domain image from Wikimedia Commons
https://www.pxfuel.com/en/free-photo-xjhmv
kiran, kumar, kiran kumar, lalithaa jewellery, lalithaa, jewellery, chennai, india, looking at camera, portrait
(images used for reference for original painting created by and modified by Peter Koren)

Unless otherwise indicated, Bible quotations are taken from New King James Version of the Bible.
Copyright © 1982 by Thomas Nelson, Inc. Used by permission. All rights reserved.
Acknowledgement to http://www.biblegateway.com/

Some of the Bible Versus that are used, significant for change and power – spirit soul and body – heart, mind and courage (body)

Colossians 1:27
27 To them God willed to make known what are the riches of the glory of this mystery among the Gentiles: which is Christ in you, the hope of glory.

Ephesians 2:10
10 For we are His workmanship, created in Christ Jesus for good works, which God prepared beforehand that we should walk in them.

John 14:6
6 Jesus said to him, "I am the way, the truth, and the life. No one comes to the Father except through Me.

Ephesians 1:17-22
17 The God of our Lord Jesus Christ, the Father of glory, may give to you the spirit of wisdom and revelation in the knowledge of Him,
18 the eyes of your understanding being enlightened; that you may know what is the hope of His calling, what are the riches of the glory of His inheritance in the saints,
19 and what is the exceeding greatness of His power toward us who believe, according to the working of His mighty power

20 which He worked in Christ when He raised Him from the dead and seated Him at His right hand in the heavenly places,
21 far above all principality and power and might and dominion, and every name that is named, not only in this age but also in that which is to come.
22 And He put all things under His feet, and gave Him to be head over all things to the church,
23 which is His body, the fullness of Him who fills all in all.

1 John 4:14-16
14 And we have seen and testify that the Father has sent the Son as Savior of the world.
15 Whoever confesses that Jesus is the Son of God, God abides in him, and he in God.
16 And we have known and believed the love that God has for us. God is love, and he who abides in love abides in God, and God in him.

Ephesians 3:14-21
14 For this reason I bow my knees to the Father of our Lord Jesus Christ,
15 from whom the whole family in heaven and earth is named,
16 that He would grant you, according to the riches of His glory, to be strengthened with might through His Spirit in the inner man,
17 that Christ may dwell in your hearts through faith; that you, being rooted and grounded in love,

18 *may be able to comprehend with all the saints what is the width and length and depth and height—*
19 *to know the love of Christ which passes knowledge; that you may be filled with all the fullness of God.*
20 *Now to Him who is able to do exceedingly abundantly above all that we ask or think, according to the power that works in us,*
21 *to Him be glory in the church by Christ Jesus to all generations, forever and ever. Amen.*

Acknowledgements for the quote and related concepts:
"Do what thou wilt"
This quote is from the law of Thelema developed by *Aleister Crowley.*
Popularised in modern culture today, but I am sure that the mindset of its proposal dates back to the beginning, at the fall of mankind.
Christian Activists and Conspiracy Theory Commentators such as:-
Tom Horn
LA Marzulli
Russ Dizdar
A must mention also is Chuck Missler and most recently Kevin Zadai particularly his Coffee Talk Series, but also check his teaching on The Son of Man, The Son of God. We do not become like Jesus a Saviour and the way, the truth and the life, but we can overcome as Jesus did as a man, submitted to God. Jesus on earth came as a man not in the form of the Son of God, He laid His life down. That's why He is our example to follow, because we must also submit to the Father, His Kingdom Come, His will be done.
These have much to say on this subject, as well as related conspiracy theories, world domination and influence in a post modern world; such as Trans Humanism, Machine and Alien, The Nephilim, The Antediluvian World, The Origin of Demons, Hybrid DNA modifications advancement to Human Being 2.0 – these reports have helped contribute to some of the related ideas, but not all of what was inspired and reflected in this book.
Also *"None Dare call it Conspiracy"* book was written by *Gary Allen.*
The above refers to mainly the Chapter "The collective consciousness of mankind".

Copyright © March 2019

Most of this book was completed in April 2014 under different titles "The Other Brother" and "Older Brother the Other" and "Brother! You didn't Earn it!" Well looks like the jury is in and "Older Brother the Other" is the winner. So this is the title that works. This latest version has extended the original message to include some more relevant messages for the times that we are living in today and our Heavenly Fathers solution for the lost and misguided sons and daughters dealing with these troubled times. The title "Older Brother the Other" uncovers our human side in relationships based on the classic parable about the prodigal son but has a focus on the attitudes of the older brother who is not impressed when his wayward brother returns and is welcomed back into the family all forgiven!!! In this book the author points us to the solution with a message of hope, recovering from the conflicts that we experience in our relationships with others during our development and the discovery of how to love people, who can be agonisingly different to us. There are also extra illustrations added, plus a new cover, the improvements have enhanced the experience of the journey that these brothers go through in the story told by this book. I am sure you will be entrenched into the brothers battles and victories with biblical teaching and references. This story is all too familiar for each of us and is pronounced by the increased measure of conflict in the world today, you read about it almost everyday in the news. Get the Good News version in the upgraded version of "Older Brother the Other."

Then there is the conspiracy scenario of what could be, first published in 2014, now we are here in 2025. Where certain Conspiracy Theories are discredited as nonsense by the mainstream, while others strangely turn out to be true.

What is a conspiracy?
To conspire, plot, scheme, create an agenda, to devise cunning plans to achieve the end game! Secret Societies and Oligarchs up to no good.
I can tell you it is all about them and not for you and me, the benefits are all one way and there is nothing in it for the people apart from false promises to deceive, coerce and then twist the truth, keep people in the dark shroud.
Do you get the meaning, something is going on and you can't always put your finger on it, see all of its working, you just sense that things are not right.
Then the evidence starts coming to light and this is not a game, they are playing for real.

We have graphene oxide inserted as a body receiver adapter, a digital interface injected, patched in the quantum tattoo.
Is it the mark? Looks a bit like it, but I don't think so the time is not yet.
Certainly it could be a prototype test run with elements of the final release.
How soon is that? Years? Decades? I don't know and this book isn't focused on that subject. Do your own research, due diligence.
God has given us the Holy Spirit to lead and guide us and show us things to come.

What is the connection to the other brother? We just followed the rabbit trail that leads us to the conclusions of man left to his own devices, rejecting God.
As Proverbs says, do not be wise in your own eyes, the way seems right to man but in the end it leads to death, pride comes before a fall.

Light Love and Peace

How did this author come to know God?
I experienced His all-encompassing, light, love and peace in an encounter when I was about 14 years old.
This happened at a time when I didn't know or believe in God and I certainly wasn't a saint.
It happened when I went to a youth group at the Lutheran Church in Shepparton, Victoria, Australia, during that time of my life.
One particular night there at the youth group a visiting speaker came and he talked to us about the Holy Spirit. Well I heard that mentioned but had no idea who or what the Holy Spirit was.

I thought if there was a God He was so far away from us, somewhere above in Heaven.

At the end of his talk he said, "I am going to ask that the Holy Spirit come" and asked us to close our eyes and just receive. So I did! What happened next changed my life forever!!! To my surprise the Holy Spirit did come, He entered my being and I saw a brilliant light, a bright white light was filling me and all around me, it was as though I was somewhere else in the light and just having an experience out of this world. In an instant I felt God's love, His love is like nothing I have ever felt or experienced before, it just fills you and overwhelms you with a love without measure and I felt the embracing love of being totally accepted by Him, right where I was at.

To add to this experience, I just knew in an instant like a download in lightning speed into my perceptions that the truth was Jesus died for my sins on the cross and now I am forever connected into His everlasting love.
Now I was not a believer in the truth of Jesus taking our sins and offering us salvation before this happened, I was a long way off from believing anything about God.
Wait there is more, to top this off, after the light and love filled my being, a peace came in like a flood of calm waters encircling me, making me feel at total ease, a peace that was bliss like nothing else on this earth and can't be compared or described, in fact none of what happened can be described fully, it was so incredible.

How does that work? I don't have a theory for that, only God knows.
Well it has been a long walk and a journey to learn how to grow up in Him and allow Him to deal with all of my baggage and life issues and become more like Jesus, life is a continual learning to yield to His purpose and His ways.

God is saying, He wants all to have this and more, if you don't know God or you feel far away from God and you may have an upbringing where you knew about God, but life has happened and that seems a long way off from where you are now, well God wants to come into your life, be part of your life, be God of your life.

I will say that for all reading this who want to receive from God, Holy Spirit come and fill their beings. I release LIGHT, I release LOVE, I release PEACE. God says just receive it, like when you were a child and wanted the best present or the best sweet ever, you just with all you got say YES, I want that.
Come Holy Spirit and fill these ones who want more of you in their life, they want to experience your love and acceptance and all that you have for them.
Light, Love and Peace.
It is yours, receive it now and forevermore.

After encountering God, you will then begin on the journey of allowing Him to come into your life and work with you to be the best you ever.

It is daily, expect miracles, expect the blessings of the Lord, but also know it is a faith walk and sometimes the journey seems long while things are shifting and moving, even though you haven't seen change yet, it is happening, as you trust the Lord and lean not on your own understanding, commit your ways to Him, He will work out all things for the good because He loves you and you and Him are working on it together. You do your part, yielding to Him and allowing Him to work, having faith that He is a Good God, giving good gifts to you at the right time as you partner with Him and come into alignment with Him as it is in Heaven, God does His part to release what was already written about you before time began, all your days will now come into alignment with the plans of Heaven. Remember Jesus already accomplished this for you on the cross, it is already done in Heaven, the way is now open for us to enter in and receive all that Heaven has for us.

We all may be a bit like the prodigal brother or sister, went our own way, did our own thing, life wasn't fair so we were going to get what we could out of it, but it led us into bad places and bad company.
Or you could relate to more like the older brother or sister, the other, you look around and no one is doing the right thing and they are getting away with it and you are going to fix this, but it made you judgmental and no matter how hard you worked for God there was no reward.

Well Gods ways are higher than our ways, He is creating One New Man from the others and the far away ones. We become new in Him. Old things have passed away, no one deserves to be saved, we missed it one way or another, Jesus died in our place and gave us His life in exchange for our old life so we could start again as a new creation and become like Him.

You know this isn't a formula, yours isn't a repeat of mine, you will have your very own connection with God. There are so many variations, hues, nuances in light and sound and atmosphere, as well as what the effects of each of these heavenly frequencies are to our hearts, minds and bodies, touching and restoring where we need it most, only the master potter knows.
For some it is a gentle sound and mood, for others it is a loud trumpet and a light show like fireworks, just allow it to flow in it's proper time and season, all in one wave or over a flowing river meandering through wonderful sights and sounds as heaven touches earth, a point of contact that transforms darkness into light, death into life, there are no words to fully express and no limitations into how it will be for everyone, each are individually made to fit into the season and time for everything under the sun.

Here is another equation from this experience that I believe just adds up right.
Light = Revelation = You just have knowledge and understanding enlightened to you.

Liberates and translates you out of darkness into His glorious Light.
Love = Acceptance = Receiving the Love of the Father and knowing you are valued.
Peace = You being the real you as one new man in Him = walking on water from above.

God gives good gifts to His children and it His will and good pleasure to give His Holy Spirit to anyone who asks, seeks and knocks on Heaven's door.

Light love and Peace to you all.

He wishes that not one would perish, God so loved the world He gave His only Son that we all might be delivered and be with Him forever. Love has no bounds and is the most powerful force in the universe.

Receive yours.

Older Brother the Other 2025 Edition is available as

978-1-0670653-4-8	Older Brother the Other 2025 Edition Paperback
978-1-0670653-5-5	Older Brother the Other 2025 Edition Kindle
978-1-0670653-6-2	Older Brother the Other 2025 Edition EPUB
978-1-0670653-7-9	Older Brother the Other 2025 Edition PDF

The following is a previous article written about the prodigal son titled *"A Long Way Off"* and is a prelude to this book.

This Book *"Older Brother the Other"* continues the Fathers purpose and unfathomable love towards all of His children, whether they be afar off or near.

A LONG WAY OFF

Copyright © March 2019

Searching for a high in life makes this a meaningful experience with a bang for your buck! We just want to feel the love for life, as there must be a road to our somewhere in the fame of our fortunes.

We get to choose right! Where we end up on life's track is our adventure and may it swing high and be an ultimate, as that is the deal of life, find some happiness and find success, in the hustle and bustle of our metropolis.
Well what happens when you feel like you have ended up a long way off from God and your pathways have taken you away somewhere where you just don't connect with Him anymore, like maybe you did in the past days of innocence, before the crossroads came to take you away for a future probability.

You may have become distant by your lifestyle and choices, headed on the track of hard knocks. Learning the hard way has its limits to what can be endured by any mortal, as the hard road burns and wears away youthful energies and hope for the future.

You may even feel like there is a huge gulf between you and God and you don't feel worthy to come back to what you know is security - feeling like you are a lowly individual that God would not consider as a priority anymore - way down on His list, due to hard and high tripping out, on the pleasures and lust for more, that never satisfies the longing in the soul. You could feel like giving up is the only option in the daily grind where there is no refuge, only a constant storm, an inner reminder saying, "*you just didn't make it and you fell off the success ladder*".

It just isn't worth trying to impress anyone anymore, too depressing to make another go of it - might as well accept defeat! No way! A hopeful voice appeals to you once again! There is a faint memory of acceptance and love and mercy from a Loving, Father God in Heaven, you know that somewhere deep inside, there is a flicker of hope, to sustain and rekindle a brand new day of acceptance and another chance, just for you and just for me - come again.

Hopelessness and despair are powerful negative emotions that can keep us from moving forward.

Our vision becomes blurred and we just can't see any way out of our dire situation and no hope in the future. When our heart sinks down low, there just isn't that spark to pull us up and project us towards some type of victory - the cards are stacked up against us and it seems like all the luck has run out on us.
Deep down there is a resilience, a smoldering ember of hope and when all looks lost, we can make a decision just to reach out to the God of all creation, who is awesome in His Love and Power.

He has made all of the bright stars in this majestic universe, where we are overwhelmed by the splendour of the bright and twinkling display lighting up in the night sky.
Still, just when you are at a point of desperation you call out for mercy, hoping that He will listen and consider your desperate appeal - you know that you really blew it big, this time.

Well the definition for sin is just that - you have missed the mark - and guess what you have fulfilled it to the full - not something to be proud of, but what can you do?

You know you have made an effort in the past, but the allure of the enticing pleasures pulled you into the net, resistance is futile it seems, it is inevitable!

Now there is no real pleasure anymore, feels like a sticky web with a huge unseen spider, waiting to completely coil you up for food. No it does not truly satisfy and it only ever gave a brief buzz, not true happiness and now you are worn down and destitute from reckless living, it is a spiral going out of control and it drags you down its slippery plug hole.

Well I can tell you - there is Good News for the lost and the far away departed.

The Father (God) saw the prodigal son who spent his inheritance on reckless living and pleasures - returning, dejected, having ended up in a pig pen - while he was returning and still a long way off and coming out of the distant places of ruin, the Father saw him.
How would the Father happen to see him when he was such a long way off?
I can tell you that it is the compassion and love of our Heavenly Father, who is our God and made us all - you and me are His creation - beloved and wonderfully made, He loves us so much, beyond our limited perceptions, that He can sense our desperation and willingness to return from our unacceptable lifestyle.

Luke 15:20 -
***"While he was still a long way off"* - *"his Father saw him"*.**
His Father saw him and filled with compassion, ran to His son and threw His arms around him. (paraphrased)

Does that sound like a God of severe judgment and the God of wrath that is all about punishing us for our sins?
Yes we do deserve it, no doubt, the punishment is due and coming to us, unless we are willing to return and give our life over to the Heavenly Father of true compassion.

Being a long way off - is a place where many of us find ourselves in the life journey and the pits that we end up in, because we are flawed and have our own agenda to live according to our own selfish desires. Where does it get us - usually in the pig pen.
Yes God is not mocked - what we sow we reap and what goes around comes around, you know there is a universal law at work.
However, we can change direction, we can change track and reverse out of the mess. And guess what! The Father runs towards us, when He sees us make that change of heart, from our place of a long way off!

It most likely will be a process of workings out, to unravel a lifetime of errors and destruction - but the decision is in an instant that can change our entire future for the good - instead of remaining in the place of total despair and doom there is a way out - spelt **JESUS** - yes the Father has made a way out of being condemned - to be redeemed - saved from ruination and destruction. Now we can freely accept this gift, without fear and we can come as we are, in the very state we are in, to be accepted.

We don't have to go through hoops and hurdles and achieve a level of holiness before we are accepted.

God knows you and all of your weaknesses and everything that you have done wrong and are going to do wrong, despite all of the mess, He still loves you and is waiting for you to come back to Him.
Stop running away from the only One who loves you where you are at, He has got it sorted, there is an answer and a free gift that will be the new life for you.

So don't worry, don't try to figure it out and make it right - just surrender to His love. Free will or your free choice will never be violated, so God isn't going to make you come, He wants you to decide and no one else can do that for you - what say you?

Come as you are - let the God who created this wonderful planet and the universe and all power do the work in you -
it is not too hard for Him, nothing makes Him hesitate or is beyond His ability.

He has put our sins as far as the east is from the west. *Psalm 103*

Don't feel that you are just not worthy enough, because what you have done is just so bad that no one would ever forgive your gross sin.

God is not limited and is infinitely greater than just anyone's ultimate bad, He is LOVE, His nature is LOVE and He never changes, it is only us that can refuse His love and miss out on His invitation.

Though you be a **long way off**, you can always turn around and begin to step towards your best future, that will be bright and full of promise.

Look towards God, who loves you and can never fail.

www.ingramcontent.com/pod-product-compliance
Lightning Source LLC
Chambersburg PA
CBHW070607010526
44118CB00012B/1466